the natural and the social

AN INTRODUCTION TO THE SOCIAL SCIENCES: UNDERSTANDING SOCIAL CHANGE

This book is part of a series produced in association with The Open University. The complete list of books in the series is as follows:

The books form part of the Open University courses DD100 and DD121/DD122 *An Introduction to the Social Sciences: Understanding Social Change*. Details of these and other Open University courses can be obtained from the Course Information and Advice Centre, PO Box 724, The Open University, Milton Keynes MK7 6ZS, United Kingdom: tel. +44 (0)1908 653231, e-mail general-enquiries@open.ac.uk

Alternatively, you may visit the Open University website at http://www.open.ac.uk where you can learn more about the wide range of courses and packs offered at all levels by The Open University.

For availability of other course components visit the webshop at www.ouw.co.uk, or contact Open University Worldwide, Michael Young Building, Walton Hall, Milton Keynes MK7 6AA, United Kingdom for a brochure. tel. +44 (0)1908 858785; fax +44 (0)1908 858787; e-mail ouwenq@open.ac.uk

the natural and the social: uncertainty, risk, change

edited by steve hinchliffe and kath woodward

London and New York

in association with

The Open University

First published 2000 by Routledge; written and produced by The Open University
Second edition 2004
11 New Fetter Lane, London EC4P 4EE

Simultaneously published in the USA and Canada by Routledge
29 West 35th Street, New York, NY 10001

Routledge is an imprint of the Taylor & Francis Group

© 2000, 2004 The Open University

This text has been printed on paper produced in Sweden from wood from managed forests using an elemental chlorine-free bleaching process. It has been stated as being environmentally friendly by the Swedish Association for the Protection of Nature.

Edited, designed and typeset by The Open University.

Printed and bound in Malta by Gutenberg Press.

British Library Cataloguing in Publication Data
A catalogue record for this book is available from The British Library

Library of Congress Cataloging in Publication Data
A catalogue record for this book has been requested

ISBN 0-415-32969-8 (hbk)

ISBN 0-415-32970-1 (pbk)

ISBN 0-203-39217-5 (ebk)

Contents

The Open University course team

John Allen, *Professor of Geography*

Penny Bennett, *Editor*

Pam Berry, *Compositor*

Simon Bromley, *Senior Lecturer in Government*

Lydia Chant, *Course Manager*

Stephen Clift, *Editor*

Allan Cochrane, *Professor of Public Policy*

Lene Connolly, *Print Buying Controller*

Jonathan Davies, *Graphic Designer*

Graham Dawson, *Lecturer in Economics*

Ross Fergusson, *Staff Tutor in Social Policy*

Fran Ford, *Senior Course Co-ordination Secretary*

Ian Fribbance, *Staff Tutor in Economics*

David Goldblatt, *Co-Course Team Chair*

Richard Golden, *Production and Presentation Administrator*

Jenny Gove, *Lecturer in Psychology*

Peter Hamilton, *Lecturer in Sociology*

Celia Hart, *Picture Researcher*

David Held, *Professor of Politics and Sociology*

Susan Himmelweit, *Professor of Economics*

Stephen Hinchliffe, *Lecturer in Geography*

Wendy Hollway, *Professor of Psychology*

Gordon Hughes, *Senior Lecturer in Social Policy*

Wendy Humphreys, *Staff Tutor in Government*

Jonathan Hunt, *Co-publishing Advisor*

Christina Janoszka, *Course Manager*

Pat Jess, *Staff Tutor in Geography*

Bob Kelly, *Staff Tutor in Government*

Margaret Kiloh, *Staff Tutor in Social Policy*

Sylvia Lay-Flurrie, *Secretary*

Gail Lewis, *Senior Lecturer in Social Policy*

Siân Lewis, *Graphic Designer*

Liz McFall, *Lecturer in Sociology*

Tony McGrew, *Professor of International Relations, University of Southampton*

Hugh Mackay, *Staff Tutor in Sociology*

Maureen Mackintosh, *Professor of Economics*

Eugene McLaughlin, *Senior Lecturer in Criminology and Social Policy*

Andrew Metcalf, *Senior Producer, BBC*

Gerry Mooney, *Staff Tutor in Social Policy*

Lesley Moore, *Senior Course Co-ordination Secretary*

Ray Munns, *Graphic Artist*

Karim Murji, *Senior Lecturer in Sociology*

Sarah Neal, *Lecturer in Social Policy*

Kathy Pain, *Staff Tutor in Geography*

Clive Pearson, *Tutor Panel*

Ann Phoenix, *Professor of Psychology*

Lynn Poole, *Tutor Panel*

Raia Prokhovnik, *Senior Lecturer in Government*

Norma Sherratt, *Staff Tutor in Sociology*

Roberto Simonetti, *Lecturer in Economics*

Dick Skellington, *Project Officer*

Brenda Smith, *Staff Tutor in Psychology*

Mark Smith, *Senior Lecturer in Government*

Matt Staples, *Course Manager*

Grahame Thompson, *Professor of Political Economy*

Ken Thompson, *Professor of Sociology*

Diane Watson, *Staff Tutor in Sociology*

Stuart Watt, *Lecturer in Psychology*

Andy Whitehead, *Graphic Artist*

Kath Woodward, *Course Team Chair, Senior Lecturer in Sociology*

Chris Wooldridge, *Editor*

External Assessor

Nigel Thrift, *Professor of Geography, University of Bristol*

Series preface

The Natural and the Social: Uncertainty, Risk, Change is the second in a series of five books, entitled *An Introduction to the Social Sciences: Understanding Social Change*. If the social sciences are to retain and extend their relevance in the twenty-first century there can be little doubt that they will have to help us understand social change. In the 1990s an introductory course to the social sciences would have looked completely different.

From a global perspective it appears that the pace of change is quickening, social and political ideas and institutions are under threat. The international landscape has changed; an intensification of technological change across computing, telecommunications, genetics and biotechnology present new political, cultural and moral dilemmas and opportunities. Real intimations of a global environmental crisis in the making have emerged. We are, it appears, living in an uncertain world. We are in new territory.

The same is also true of more local concerns. At the beginning of the twenty-first century both societies and the social sciences are in a state of flux. *Understanding Social Change* has been written at a moment that reflects, albeit in a partial way, subterranean shifts in the social and cultural character of the UK. Established social divisions and social identities of class, gender, ethnicity and nation are fragmenting and re-forming. Core institutions such as the family, work and welfare have become more diverse and complex. It is also a moment when significant processes of change have been set in train – such as constitutional reform and European economic and monetary union – whose longer-term trajectory remains uncertain. The flux in the social sciences has been tumultuous. Social change, uncertainty and diversity have rendered many of the most well-established frameworks in the social sciences of limited use and value. Social change on this scale demands fresh perspectives and new systems of explanation.

In this context *Understanding Social Change* is part of a bold and innovative educational project, for it attempts to capture and explore these processes of momentous social change and in doing so reasserts the utility and necessity of the social sciences. Each of the five books which make up the series attempts precisely this, and they all do so from a fundamentally interdisciplinary perspective. Social change is no respecter of the boundaries of disciplines and the tidy boxes that social scientists have often tried to squeeze it into. Above all, *Understanding Social Change* seeks to maintain and extend the Open University's democratic educational mission: to reach and enthuse an enormously diverse student population; to insist that critical, informed, reflexive engagement with the direction of social change is not a matter for elites and professional social scientists alone.

As you may have guessed, this series of books forms a core component of the Open University, Faculty of Social Sciences, level 1 course, DD100 *An Introduction to the Social Sciences: Understanding Social Change*. Each book in the series can be read independently of the other books and independently from the rest of the materials that make up the Open University course. However, if you wish to use the series as a whole, there are a number of references to chapters in other books in the series, and these are easily identifiable because they are printed in bold type.

Making the course and these books has been a long and complex process, and thanks are due to an enormous number of people.

First and foremost, the entire project has been managed and kept on the rails, when it was in mortal danger of flying off them, by our excellent Course Manager, Christina Janoszka. In the DD100 office, Fran Ford, Lesley Moore and Sylvia Lay-Flurrie have been the calm eye at the centre of a turbulent storm, our thanks to all of them. For the second edition we have had the much valued support of Matt Staples and Lydia Chant.

Stephen Clift, Chris Wooldridge and Penny Bennett have been meticulous, hawk-eyed editors. Siân Lewis has provided superb design work, and Ray Munns and Andy Whitehead have provided skilled cartographic and artistic work. David Calderwood and then Richard Golden in project control have arranged and guided the schedule with calm efficiency and Celia Hart has provided great support with illustrations and photographs. Nigel Thrift, our external assessor, and Clive Pearson, Elizabeth Chaplin and Lynne Poole, our tutor panel, provided consistent and focused criticism, support and advice. Peggotty Graham has been an invaluable friend of *Understanding Social Change* and David Held provided balance, perspective and insight as only he can.

It only remains for us to say that we hope you find *Understanding Social Change* an engaging and illuminating introduction to the social sciences, and in turn you find the social sciences essential for understanding life in the twenty-first century.

David Goldblatt
Kath Woodward
Co-Chairs, The Open University Course Team

Introduction

Steve Hinchliffe and Kath Woodward

This book is about the ways in which society and nature combine. You may be used to thinking that society and nature, almost by definition, are matters to be kept apart. Indeed, in our everyday language, we tend to treat nature and society as opposites. If something is described as natural, then we tend to think that it is unlikely to have much to do with society. So, for example, when we describe a landscape as 'natural' we often mean to suggest that it is undeveloped, untouched and that the social world is largely absent. When we talk about someone having a natural talent (for music or sport, say), then we tend to imply that they were born with it. The social worlds of education and training are almost thought to be irrelevant to the way in which we judge their particular 'gift'.

To think like this is to think of the social and the natural as separate or pure categories. It is almost as if they are different objects, with neat boundaries and no overlap. We can call this way of thinking about the social and the natural a *purified* approach. Figure 1 is a schematic representation of this purified view.

FIGURE 1   Nature and society as pure categories

This book sets out to challenge this purified view of nature and society. Each of the chapters deals with different topics, from what we mean by 'human nature' (Chapter 1), to health care and medicine (Chapter 2), to markets and pollution (Chapter 3), to natural hazards and food scares (Chapter 4). One way of thinking about the book's structure is that we move from 'inner nature' (bodies, personalities and what makes us human) to 'outer nature' (the environments and the non-human world within which we live and co-exist with other people, plants and animals). Common to all the chapters is an attempt to break down the assumed boundaries between nature and society. Indeed, the conviction is that the categories of nature and society are impossible to hold apart when we engage with the real worlds in which people live.

This breaking down of boundaries might seem counter-intuitive. So here are two examples to start you thinking about nature and society interrelationships.

1   Cloning Ryan Giggs

   After a series of bad results, the Welsh football manager joked that he wouldn't mind a clone or two of his star player, Ryan Giggs. Giggs is a player with natural talent, a player with a gift, a player born with a special set of genes. Now, joking apart, what would it mean to really produce an exact replica of Ryan Giggs? Is it simply a matter of taking a few cells from his body, extracting the genetic material and inserting it into an unfertilized egg? If we then transfer this egg into a surrogate mother, will the organism that develops really be another Welsh international footballer? Is there more to him than that?

What about Giggs's upbringing, would that matter? Can we really treat his body and the body of his surrogate mother as pure nature? Will his mother's pregnancy be important? Will she eat the right foods, do the right exercises and get the right treatment? How will he be fed, looked after and educated? Does the intensive training provided by his football club, Manchester United – one of the richest in the world – matter? If we were truly serious about a Ryan Giggs clone, then wouldn't we have to provide a copy of all or most of his (and his pregnant mother's) interactions with other people, organizations and institutions? In other words, isn't Ryan Giggs a human being who has a social as well as a natural life? (Try not to let your preconceptions about football players or the team you support colour your answer.) In this book we will argue that when we talk about people's identities and lives, it doesn't really make much sense to tease the natural and the social apart.

2   Natural parks?

Now look at the photograph in Figure 2 of Snowdonia National Park. Would you say it was a natural or a social scene? In many ways it looks to be untouched by social worlds. But on closer inspection there are signs that this scene is as social as it is natural.

FIGURE 2   Snowdonia National Park: a natural or a social landscape?

For example, the grasses and peaty soils are the result of thousands of years of human involvement in the land. Much of this land has been deforested in the past two thousand years and used for grazing sheep. If the sheep were removed, under present climatic conditions, the landscape would soon be dominated by scrub. The sheep are domesticated breeds that owe their form to generations of selective breeding. They are not just domesticates (which literally means brought into the house, or we could say 'socialized'), they are also commodities. Their status as marketable products is linked into a whole range of social institutions. These include land and property rights (notice the fence running across the landscape), currency markets, the Ministry of Agriculture, the European Commission, the radiation from the nearby nuclear power station, wholesalers, supermarkets, consumers of lamb meat and wool products, and production and transportation economies that link this scene to places as far away as New Zealand. All of these are tied into the Snowdonia scene in various ways and at various times by virtue of their connection to hill sheep farming. And the connections can shift in ways that can change our 'natural' scene. For example, as financial subsidies to farmers are cut, as dietary habits change and as imports become cheaper, the economics of hill sheep farming in areas like Snowdonia may become more marginal and precarious.

If the economics of hill sheep farming become any more marginal than they already are, then the landscape might change very radically indeed. In order to preserve this scene, the National Park authorities, the National Trust and other organizations will not only have to protect wildlife and vegetation, they will also have to protect the farmers and their livelihoods. To do so, money will need to be raised from elsewhere. The ability to raise money will partly depend on the wider population valuing this scene. In sum, the ecology of this scene not only includes the plants, animals and climate of North Wales, it also includes a wide range of equally changeable social and economic relations.

These examples may have convinced you that nature and society are indeed two sides of the same coin. The following four chapters will contain further examples and issues that should convince you even further. We can now state our first major aim of this book. It is largely inspired by feminist social sciences (Franklin *et al.*, 2000) and also by the work of the French sociologist Bruno Latour (1993).

Aim 1: To demonstrate that nature and society are rarely if ever purely natural or purely social. The social and the natural exist in mixes.

However, we won't stop there. The aim of the book is not simply to demonstrate the entangled character of nature and society. Our second aim is to suggest that this demonstration of impurity is both useful and necessary at the current time. At the beginning of a new millennium, we are faced with increasing evidence that our attempts to understand nature and society as pure categories (Figure 1) no longer suits our world. We could not, for example, see an easy way to manage the environment in Snowdonia without understanding something of the nature and society mix that exists in this part of Wales. Nor could we hope to make an informed decision about the implications for human beings of new genetic technologies without understanding the social and natural mix that goes into being human. In short, in this world where risks and uncertainties seem to be piling up on top of one another, we need ways of understanding that refuse to purify the world into nature on the one hand and society on the other. If we are to make improvements to people's lives, not to mention other species' lives, then any attempts to understand nature without society, or to understand society without nature, will prove insufficient to the task. We can now state our second aim.

Aim 2: To demonstrate the importance of considering nature and society together at a point in time when we seem to be faced with ever increasing uncertainty and risk.

The final aim of the book is to demonstrate that the social sciences provide some of the most promising vantage points from where we can start this difficult task of thinking about nature and society as two sides of the same coin. Too often, it seems, environmental and bio-medical questions are left to 'scientific' experts. This is particularly the case in Britain. The result is that we approach nature and society questions by either ignoring society altogether, or by using models of society that are out of date or grossly simplified. This book, therefore, contains a significant amount of work that will introduce you to some of the approaches and techniques that are used in the social sciences. Likewise, the text is written so as to emphasize the ways in which social scientists develop arguments by engaging with different kinds of evidence. So here is our third and final aim.

Aim 3: To demonstrate the resources and skills that social scientists can bring to social and natural issues and debates.

In Chapter 1, Wendy Hollway asks what it means to be a human being, looking at the similarities and differences between and within species. These ideas are developed by examining different accounts, for example some scientific as well as social scientific accounts, which have been developed at different times, historically. The chapter goes on to address the question of what is human nature, by looking at some specific aspects of human experience, namely sexuality and death and by considering a range of approaches to finding out about 'human nature'. This focus on inner nature continues in Chapter 2 where Brenda Smith and David Goldblatt discuss health and illness. The chapter takes you through various ways in which our bodies and health are understood. Behind each of these is a different understanding of nature and society relations and the authors demonstrate how each has its successes and failures. Through a history of British health policy, Brenda and David also demonstrate how our approach to inner nature and health is bound into particular versions of society. The current emphasis given to lifestyle and risk, which on the face of it sounds as though it manages to integrate social and environmental issues, is linked to a broader move in society to individualize responsibility for health. The integration of environment and society is taken up in Chapter 3, where Sue Himmelweit and Roberto Simonetti discuss the role of markets in the production of environmental degradation. As they are currently organized, markets tend to place no value on large areas of life that we have become used to calling nature. The authors demonstrate in detail why this under-valuing occurs and then critically examine the kinds of policies that economists have devised to deal with the problem. They argue that integrating nature and society may be possible through market adjustments, but we need to be careful to consider the political as well as the economic implications when we try to implement these policies. Finally, in Chapter 4, Steve Hinchliffe takes a more explicit look at living with risk. The argument in this chapter is that risk is often intensified when nature and society are considered as separate matters. He argues that the only way to improve our chances and live with risk more effectively is to seek ways of successfully combining nature and society in our understanding and in our practices. Steve Hinchliffe uses examples from around the world, including natural disasters and food scares, to illustrate the argument.

Each chapter develops its own approach to society and nature issues. The result is a breadth of treatments and approaches. Uniquely, we range over a wide territory, not content to limit ourselves to inner nature or to what are more conventionally called environmental questions. We move from genes to planet earth and back again. In doing so we hope to demonstrate the interconnections between these subject matters and between the various social scientific approaches that we take to them.

References

Franklin, S., Lury, C. and Stacey, J. (eds) (2000) *Global Nature, Global Culture*, London, Sage.

Latour, B. (1993) *We Have Never Been Modern*, London, Harvester Wheatsheaf.

What is human nature?

Wendy Hollway

chapter 1

Contents

1 INTRODUCTION

If you have stopped to think about the title of this chapter, you may already be wondering what you mean when you use a phrase such as 'it's only human nature after all'. When you say 'it's in my nature', what do you mean by it? Probably you are referring to a part of your personality or behaviour that you feel is unchangeable. This is one of the main uses of the idea of nature in everyday language: it refers to all those parts of human behaviour that are regarded as fixed, inherent or innate.

The Oxford English Dictionary's primary definition of nature reflects this meaning: 'the inherent and innate disposition or character of a person (or animal)'. This core meaning relies on an implicit comparison with characteristics that are not innate, that is, acquired characteristics. Here we see the opposition between what is natural and what is social. People often assume that human beings are born in a state of nature. Indeed, the word nature comes from the Latin 'nasci', meaning to be born. The main topic of this book is to examine the categories of 'natural' and 'social' and to show how these interconnect and are better understood as two sides of the same coin. The topic of human nature invites us to look at the way these two categories interact. When, for example, someone uses the refrain 'it's only human nature' they are frequently invoking human nature in order to excuse the behaviour of someone who has broken society's rules. The bad behaviour might be of a violent or sexually inappropriate kind and it may seek to be excused on the grounds that they could not help it. These modes of behaviour are thought of as human nature breaking out – undesirably but inevitably – into a person's conduct when that person does not exercise sufficient control over 'natural' impulses.

Why is the word 'natural' in inverted commas here? They are used when words are quoted from another source or when they are put around a name of something. A further common usage of inverted commas is to suggest that what the word is describing cannot be taken at face value. If you were speaking such an idea out loud you would probably say 'so-called natural' to convey the same idea. Social science involves asking questions about what is meant when we use terms such as natural. For this purpose it is useful to question our own common-sense usage and also – as in this chapter – to look at changes in the use of an idea over time. By the end of the chapter, it should be clear that it is misleading to suppose that something such as sexually aggressive behaviour is in any simple and direct way the expression of natural human behaviour.

To excuse behaviour because it is supposed to be an unavoidable expression of something innate also demonstrates the relevance of the topic of human nature for debates about agency and structure. Does human agency (choice) govern behaviour or does a natural structure, such as human nature, dictate how we behave? In this chapter I argue for going beyond the idea that it has to be either one or the other, just as I try to show that arguing that human behaviour is either natural or social is unhelpful because it blinds us to the way that these inevitably interact.

What is considered to be the most 'natural' set of activities that humans display? I use two main examples in this chapter: dying and sex. We shall look at the arguments for these being both natural and social events to provide examples of how these two categories are misleading when understood as separate.

I begin with a brief history that illuminates why the question 'what is human nature?' is important. Section 2 summarizes the key idea of Christian thought that dominated in Europe for centuries until challenged by a scientific way of thinking about human nature. This idea was that humans were placed by the creator in a 'great chain of being', nearer to God than they were to animals. History shows that different answers to the question have very different implications for politics and the way that powerful groups treat others. This is the topic of Section 3. In Section 4, I provide a summary of the main argument of evolutionary theory and explain why it necessitated such a radical transformation of ideas about human nature. Western beliefs about why and how humans were different from (superior to) other animals had to be rethought. This raised new questions about what humans have in common as a species and therefore also what accounts for differences among groups. There are still no settled answers, in biological, psychological or social sciences. Section 5 is about how science has approached the question of human nature since Darwin. In contrast, Section 6 looks at social science approaches to human nature, starting with the example of human burial. It encompasses social and psychological approaches. Section 7 takes the example of human sexuality to show how it is possible to integrate biological, social and psychological approaches to human nature.

The main purpose of this chapter is to enable you to think about human nature in a way that goes beyond common sense. In order to do this I introduce you to several major perspectives from which to view human nature:

- Historical and political perspectives (Sections 2 and 3)

- A scientific perspective, including evolutionary, genetic and palaeontological accounts (Sections 4 and 5)

- Social accounts emphasizing the importance of social relations, culture and symbols (Section 6)

- Psychological accounts, including a developmental perspective, on intersubjectivity, self-consciousness, imagination and being-in-time (Section 6).

2 HUMAN NATURE IN EUROPEAN HISTORY

There is a tension in the phrase 'human nature' because its two words link together the human with the natural and yet the natural is understood to be that which all living creatures share. This is illustrated in the Old Testament of the Christian bible. The Old Testament is a relevant place to begin because the Judaeo-Christian tradition is so dominant in European, North American and, more generally, Western culture. Importantly, it has influenced the development of **modernity**, in particular through science, in a way that no corner of the world has escaped.

Modernity

Modernity is the period of history that started with the development of science, technology and industry in Europe around the seventeenth century. It is characterized by a belief in the possibility of controlling nature to ensure progress. Social scientists are engaged in a debate about whether this period is giving way to post-modernity, a period where belief in certainties is collapsing and being replaced by many competing claims to knowledge and a lack of authority to decide amongst them.

ACTIVITY 1.1

The following passage is from Psalm 8 in the Old Testament: 'What is Man, that Thou art mindful of him? ... Thou hast made him a little lower than the angels, and hast crowned him with glory and honour.'

Jot down some answers to these four questions before you read on.

- How do you make sense of this passage, which comes from a way of thinking that is quite unfamiliar to most contemporary readers?
- Who is the passage addressed to and what has this figure achieved?
- What can we glean about how the Judaeo-Christian tradition saw human nature?
- What is the main purpose of this passage?

COMMENT

The passage is addressed to God. In it God is the creator of Man and had a definite purpose in so doing. More broadly, therefore, we can say that questions about human nature were seen in a religious light: the reason for humans being on the earth was explicable by God's purpose. Likewise, every other world religion has had its own account of human nature in terms of its own God or Gods. You may also have noticed that the question of human nature was cast in terms of the masculine pronoun: him not her, man not woman. We shall come back to the persistent tendency in Western thought to differentiate between the sexes when human nature is under consideration.

By using the phrase 'a little lower', 'Man' is placed in a hierarchy only just below the angels and therefore granted special features by God that result in glory and honour. The general effect of the passage on believers would therefore be to cast human beings in a very favourable light. Moreover, by implication, the status of Man in this hierarchy is achieved by comparing him not only to the angels but to what came lower down: Man is being compared to animals and found considerably superior. Here we see an example of the way that human nature is tied to animal nature in Western thought.

The hierarchy that put human beings in between the angels and animals is referred to as 'the great chain of being' an illustration of which you can see in Figure 1.1 (overleaf). It was understood as the order established by God, the creator, an order in which varieties of living beings were arranged in small gradations from the simplest of animals upwards. These groups had fixed characteristics, given by God. Any species could thus be compared to any other.

For centuries this was the European way of understanding where human beings fitted into life and how to define their status. One of the themes in contemporary social science is that dominant ideas – whether scientific or not – serve a social function that is never neutral in its effects. Placing humans high up in the creator's chain of being served to define them as having a special status and thereby to justify their domination over other creatures. This is an example of a political perspective: it understands the history of human nature in the light of theories about power relations. We shall take up this theme in the following section where we see that only some people – European men of the 'rational' kind – were thought to qualify as having reached the heights of humankind.

As you will see, when science replaced religion as the dominant way of knowing, it took as central the task of defining the difference between human and non-human animals. You will find that a recurrent theme in this chapter is the strong need in Western culture to understand humans as different from other animals. Just think of the way in which animals are called 'dumb beasts'. It is derogatory and centres on animals' lack of language and, by implication, the stupidity that is often assumed to be a consequence. On the other hand, such a position has often been challenged. In 1619, Italian philosopher Lucilio Vanini was burned alive for suggesting that humans evolved from apes.

ACTIVITY 1.2

What distinguishes humans from other animals? Make a list of three distinguishing characteristics.

COMMENT _____

Some answers to this question, and a discussion of them, appear at the beginning of Section 5. Keep a note of your answers, which will be useful when you get to Section 5. What animal did you have in mind when you thought about the comparison with humans? It is likely that you thought of chimpanzees because they are frequently used for this purpose as the species which is closest to human beings.

FIGURE 1.1 'The Great Chain of Being', from Didacus Valades, *Rhetorica Christiana*, 1579

Matthew Arnold, the Victorian English poet, saw the relationship between humans and animals as follows:

> Know, man hath all which Nature hath, but more,
> And in that *more* lie all his hopes of good.
>
> (cited in Jahoda, 1992, p.190)

There is a lot condensed in these two lines of poetry in which Matthew Arnold expressed a common hope of the time in Europe. Having allowed that man and nature share a set of natural characteristics, he expresses the opinion that it is *not* in these that all good lies, but rather in what is beyond them, in that 'more' (original emphasis). If all good lies in what is not nature, then logically where does all bad lie? It must lie in nature. The implication, then, is the closer to nature, the less good. Arnold was contrasting nature (understood as instinct or impulse) with the civilized virtues that enabled man to overcome and control nature: the virtues of mind such as rationality, self-control, appreciation of beauty. These values were typical of the Victorian era (Queen Victoria reigned in Britain from 1837 to 1901). In the nineteenth century, Nature and Mind were treated as opposites. During the twentieth century, the emphasis increasingly was placed on the external influences on Mind and the opposition became one of Nature and Culture. In this book we use the terms 'natural' and 'social' to refer to what is essentially the same opposition.

Sigmund Freud's thought, developed initially in the late nineteenth century, provides a good example of theory that sees a conflict between the natural and the social. Freudian psychoanalysis was built on the idea that being human is defined by the conflict between instincts (the natural) and the restraining forces of civilization (the cultural and social) (Freud, 1920/1955). What is important about Freud's thinking is that these social influences did not directly or automatically shape the instincts and civilize or socialize people. For Freud, what distinguishes human beings from animals is humans' ability to deny and repress their natural drives or instincts, in particular the drive to seek out instant gratification (the pleasure principle), and re-channel the energies that derive from them into cultural activities. Civilization – art, science, technology and religion – depends on the repression of our pleasure-seeking drive (Freud, 1930/1961). Repression creates desire. Thus the conflict between the natural and the social is enacted internally by individuals, shaping their personalities. What defines *human* nature, according to Freud, was repression of natural drives and its consequences, which he saw as shaping human destiny.

In summary, Freud believed that the conflict between the natural and the social is enacted both within individuals, as an internal mental conflict, and also among individuals in their social relations. This psychological conflict is one of the features that distinguishes human nature from animal nature.

SUMMARY

- In Europe, until the rise of science in the eighteenth and nineteenth centuries, a Judaeo-Christian religious perspective understood human nature as the creation of God.
- The religious idea of the creator's 'great chain of being' placed man close to the angels and considerably higher than animals.
- It was common to see human virtues as deriving from what was not natural or animal.
- For Freud, human nature was based on the idea of a psychological conflict between instinct (the natural) and civilization (the social).

3 THE CIVILIZED AND OTHERS IN THE EMERGENCE OF SCIENCE

By the end of the seventeenth century, nature was no longer treated in Europe primarily as a force to be respected as being more powerful than mere human beings. The project of the emerging sciences was to understand, and therefore be able to control, the forces of nature. The scientists in charge of this project were the manifestation of 'Mind' that stood in opposition to nature. However, the model of the scientist was male. Now guess what gender nature was associated with: female of course! Did the phrase 'mother nature' spring to mind? It is still in common use. Evidently science was associated with what was masculine and nature was conceptualized as feminine.

Nature was not just associated with motherhood, through their shared fertility. Nature was also the force that man could tame and control. Francis Bacon, a scientist writing early in the seventeenth century, made clear the close association between scientific knowledge and power just as science was emerging in Europe. He associated these with masculinity. Consider the following metaphors used by Bacon to characterize science and its relation to nature. He referred to 'a chaste and lawful marriage between Mind and Nature'. He used a notion of feminine servitude too: 'I am come in very truth leading you to Nature with all her children to bind her to your service and make her your slave'. At other times Bacon saw science's relationship to nature as characterized by a more violent form of power: 'the power to conquer and subdue her, to shake her to her foundation'. These metaphors suggest that 'man' was not just a convenient shorthand for 'humankind' but that it was men, not women, who were seen as having the superior capabilities of Mind that could overcome the natural forces and urges that threatened civilization.

Women are still widely seen as being closer to nature than men, but they are not the only category of 'others' who were believed to be inferior by virtue of not belonging to the dominant group. The others included all non-European peoples, who were thought to occupy a lower place in the chain of being. Figure 1.2 illustrates one attempt from 1799 to grade human beings and animals. The hierarchy starts at the bottom left and ascends to the top right. The principle of gradation being used is the angle of the front profile of the head. This is given in degrees. Current language usage reflects these ideas. For example, the French word for people from non-European cultures is 'naturels' ('primitives' in English), so appealing directly to the idea of nature being the opposite of (European) culture and civilization.

From the sixteenth century, European nations were conquering territories and peoples throughout the 'new' world. The Spanish conquistadores regarded native Americans as mere beasts and so justified their inhumane treatment. There was, however, a debate about their status, which understandably at the time had to be referred to the church. Eventually the Pope pronounced native Americans to be human, but only after long deliberation. Later, when Europeans arrived in Africa and proceeded to place in their scheme of human nature the indigenous peoples they encountered, the Pygmies were placed in the middle of the chain of being, well below Europeans.

These are shocking examples of European power to subordinate other peoples. For the purposes of our interest in human nature, however, the important point is that the dominant way that human nature was known in Europe enabled other groups to be thought of as closer to nature and therefore less civilized. This in turn legitimated unequal, if not brutal, treatment.

As the influence of the church waned, what took the place of religious knowledge? The example of Francis Bacon has already given you the answer: science. Science was a revolutionary mode of thinking that transformed Western culture over the following centuries.

An entrenched account of human nature, such as the creator's chain of being, does not fade away in mere decades or even centuries, in particular when the justification of Europe's empires rested on the idea of the superiority of its own people. Whereas in the early days of colonization the view of non-Europeans derived from religious ways of knowing about human nature, gradually the emerging sciences became engaged in this question. Their focus on differences among racial groups supported the old idea that, since some racial groups were closer to non-human species than to Man, those racial groups should not be admitted to the same human status as Europeans.

Scientists, like human beings in general, can be drawn towards arguments that reinforce their own beliefs. If the qualities of Mind in males and Europeans were 'naturally' superior, the early scientists reasoned (who were themselves members of the group in whose 'superior' brains they had an

FIGURE 1.2   In 1799, Charles White made these illustrations which were published in *An Account of the Regular Gradation in Man, and in Different Animals and Vegetables*

interest), then perhaps this could be proven by measuring the size of a skull, which housed the brain. Have you noticed a problem in this logic? It assumes that the brain and the mind are the same thing. It is important to remember that the brain is a physical organ and the mind refers to a set of processes that enable thought.

Scientists who studied skulls based much of their work on comparing skull size, not between individuals, but between human groups. Men's and women's skull sizes were compared and it was claimed that the results showed that women were inferior to men in mental ability. Likewise, the skulls of Africans were claimed to be comparatively smaller than Europeans'. There are many grounds for contesting this kind of science, too numerous to detail here. Such findings have been rigorously challenged and discredited. In the twentieth century, the arguments lived on but the ways of knowing changed. Measures of the supposedly innate superiority of Mind shifted from the biological (brain measured by skull size), to the psychological ('intelligence' measured by IQ tests).

The use of these examples demonstrates how political disagreements about 'race' have been argued out on the terrain of a science of human nature. These kinds of arguments were influential, but they were also challenged. The challengers were interested in defining what different groups had in common, as human. Where they found differences, they sought the reasons in different environments, including, especially, the social environment. Nearly two centuries ago the debate was already trapped in ways of thinking that saw the influences as *either* natural *or* social, and assumed that these two things could be simply distinguished from each other when looking at human beings. This either–or position is called dualism, specifically here the dualism between natural and social, often referred to as 'nature–nurture'. You can now see that the debates between those arguing that nature determines human behaviour and those arguing for social, or cultural, influences as being determinant, have been around for a long time.

SUMMARY

- The 'civilized' European male was the model against which others, in particular women and non-Europeans, were judged to be inferior and closer to animal nature.

- The idea of a hierarchy, as in 'the great chain of being', influenced early scientists' attempts to categorize other races as in between Europeans and animals and these provided continued justification for inhuman treatment of colonized peoples.

4 EVOLUTIONARY THEORY

In this climate of scientific experimentation and intellectual debate, Charles Darwin's thought was formed. His book, entitled *On the Origin of Species by Means of Natural Selection*, published in 1859, launched the theory of evolution that produced a radical challenge to the religious account of the place of Man in nature. In place of the creator's chain of being was offered a theory about the close relationship of human and non-human animals, backed by the considerable authority that science enjoyed at that time. Darwin's argument was that **Homo sapiens** and species of great ape, such as chimpanzees, were descended from the same ape-like primate ancestor.

Homo sapiens
The Latin term *Homo sapiens* is the species name for human beings. Homo (man) sapiens (knowing or understanding) thus defines the human species by its capacity to understand or know.

By the end of the nineteenth century, Western culture was faced with convincing scientific evidence that humans were, in this crucial respect, animals. Since then, in Western thought, evolutionary theory has largely usurped the earlier idea of human nature as the gift of God.

In the evolutionary view, life does not require a purpose to explain it. It does not need a God as creator. Creatures were not designed for some end. For Darwin there was no such grand plan. These principles meant that the introduction of evolutionary theory into European thought had revolutionary implications for religious belief. The idea that species evolved went against Christian doctrine (that was why Lucilio Vanini was burned alive) in which each species had a fixed and immutable nature. The question of what is distinctive about human nature thus took on new significance: if humans are not designed to be different from animals and fixed in that difference, what differentiates us from these, our closest evolutionary relatives? Is a human being just a 'Naked Ape' (to use the title of a popular book by Desmond Morris)? On the other hand, what makes us different from apes? What makes us human?

WEDNESDAY.]   THE HORNET.   [MARCH 22ND, 1871.

A VENERABLE ORANG-OUTANG.
A CONTRIBUTION TO UNNATURAL HISTORY.

FIGURE 1.3   Darwin caricatured as an ape, published in *The Hornet*, 1871

The conflict between the teachings of the Christian bible and evolutionary theory is still politically alive at the beginning of the twenty-first century. In certain states of the USA, the teaching of evolutionary theory is only allowed if it is balanced by the religious story of creation in the book of Genesis. This account of creation says that God created all other creatures in five days, and created Man on the sixth. In other words it states that human beings were a creation distinct from other animals. It also claims, in opposition to evolutionary theory, that the world was created only a few thousand years ago. This

---

BOX I.I   **The main argument in Darwin's evolutionary theory**

- Individuals can be grouped together into species on the basis of such characteristics as shape, anatomy, physiology, behaviour and so on. These groupings are not entirely artificial: members of the same species, if reproducing sexually, can by definition breed with each other to produce fertile offspring.

- Within a species, individuals are not all identical. They will differ in physical and behavioural characteristics.

- Some of these differences are inherited from the previous generation and may be passed on to the next.

- Variation is enriched by the occurrence of spontaneous but random novelty. A feature may appear that was not present in previous generations, or may be present to a different degree.

- Resources required by organisms to thrive and reproduce are not infinite. Competition must inevitably arise, and some organisms will leave fewer offspring than others.

- Some variations will confer an advantage on their possessors in terms of access to these resources and hence in terms of leaving offspring.

- Those variants that leave more offspring will tend to be preserved and gradually become the norm. If the departure from the original ancestor is sufficiently radical, new species may form, and natural selection will have brought about evolutionary change.

- As a consequence of natural selection, organisms will become adapted to their environments in the broadest sense of being well suited to the essential processes of life such as obtaining food, avoiding predation, finding mates, competing with rivals for limited resources and so on.

(Cartwright, 2000, p.33)

---

position is called 'creationism'. Creationism has become an issue for political debate again in Europe. In *The Guardian* (9 March 2002), the head teacher of a north of England school is quoted as arguing that 'to teach children that they are nothing more than developed mutations who evolved from something akin to a monkey and that death is the end of everything is hardly going to engender within them a sense of purpose, self-worth and self-respect'. He is quoted as writing 'We agree that [schools] should teach evolution as a theory and a faith position ... Clearly also schools should teach the creation theory as literally depicted in Genesis. ... Ultimately both creation and evolution are faith positions.' Richard Dawkins, Professor of the Public Understanding of Science at the University of Oxford, commented in reply as follows: 'Creation as literally depicted in Genesis is indeed supported by faith (and needs to be, since it is not supported by anything else) ... Evolution, on the other hand, is supported by evidence.'

Darwin's theory made sense of the observations he had painstakingly made about a vast variety of plant and animal species. However, he had no

Genotype
The genetic constitution of an individual.

Genes
The element that governs the development of hereditary characteristics in offspring.

evidence about what mechanism might be responsible for natural selection. By the end of the twentieth century, the science of genetics could provide an account of that mechanism. It could claim that a person's **genotype** is the biological mechanism for inheritance, that is the passing of characteristics from one generation to the next. In answer to the question why are we (human beings) here, on earth, a modern Darwinian, informed by genetics, is likely to answer that we are here because we carry genes that have been successful at self-replication in the environments in which *Homo sapiens* lived. The function of **genes** is to copy themselves. The copying is not always accurate so that, as we saw in Box 1.1, variation within a species is enriched by spontaneous, random novelty and some of these variations confer competitive advantage.

Developments in the science of genetics have provided a compelling account of the biological mechanism by which natural selection works, by which species evolve. Genes are popular candidates when people look for the seat of human nature. However, although they clearly are the crucial mechanism of the reproduction of the human species, genes do not specify or determine behaviour.

Genes set some parameters on what that individual or that species can achieve. For example, the approximate size and structure of the human brain, as laid down in human DNA, provides for language capacity in humans. It does not, however, ensure that all humans born with an intact brain will be able to use language to communicate with others. For this to happen, the genetic potential has to interact with various aspects of the physical and social environment. The physical environment must provide adequate nutrition, for example. The social environment provides the language-using interactions that normally ensure that a child will learn language (see the example in Section 6.3). These environmental influences affect the brain too.

SUMMARY

- Darwin's evolutionary theory challenged the belief in a fixed separation of human and animal species by arguing that *Homo sapiens* and species of great ape were descended from the same, ape-like, primate ancestors.

- This principle contradicted creationist religious beliefs in a way that is still contested in the USA and Europe today.

- The twentieth-century science of genetics explained the mechanism of inheritance and the means by which species evolve.

- A person's genes do not specify or determine their behaviour.

5 HUMAN NATURE ACCORDING TO SCIENCE

Darwin's evolutionary theory provided the impetus for natural scientists interested in the question of human nature. He addressed directly the question posed in Activity 1.2: what distinguishes humans from other animals? His answer was fourfold: tool use, language, an aesthetic sense and religious ardour. In this section I shall summarize the knowledge that has been produced within this scientific perspective, using Darwin's ideas about tool use and language as a starting point. (The other two – an aesthetic sense and religious ardour – have been taken up more by philosophers than scientists.) This series introduces the different sets of assumptions underlying scientific and, for example, religious knowledge (**Woodward and Watt, 2004**; **Thompson and Woodward, 2004**). Here it is useful simply to say that scientific knowledge is based on a belief that 'facts' – reliable and certain knowledge – can be discovered through the systematic use of scientific methods. Others contend that scientific knowledge, like religious knowledge (the belief in the great chain of being, for example), is affected by time, place and power relations.

5.1 Tool use

Tool use has emerged as important through studies using an evolutionary perspective of the great apes with whom *Homo sapiens* once shared a common ancestor (one that died out about seven million years ago). It is thought that when ancestors of *Homo sapiens* evolved to walk on two rather than four legs, this freed up their front limbs to specialize for different purposes. From a front foot on which to move around, hands developed and, importantly, thumb and forefinger evolved so that they opposed one another and permitted the manipulation of objects. It is widely argued that this was a crucial adaptation because it enabled *Homo sapiens*' ancestors to become tool users. The whole of technology has developed out of rudimentary tool use. It is now well documented that chimps commonly use sticks for extracting termites from nests to eat. They use appropriately shaped stones as hammers and move stones into places where they can be stepped on to reach food. They also chew up leaves for the purpose of soaking up water from places otherwise unreachable. Scientists agree, therefore, that elementary tool use has evolved in other species, notably chimpanzees and gorillas, and that although tool use is not therefore a defining characteristic of human nature, it is significant in the evolution of the great apes with whom *Homo sapiens* shared a common ancestor.

BOX 1.2   **Scientific methods for studying human nature**

What sort of methods can support or challenge this account of tool use and the following account of the evolution of language?

- Ethologists observing animal behaviour in the wild have recorded and filmed modern primates' use of tools. (Ethology: the study of animals in their natural habitat.)
- Since the mid nineteenth century, a great deal of scientific evidence has been collected about the evolution of primate species based on skeletons and fossil remains. This area of study is called palaeontology.
- The dating of fossil and skeletal remains used to be quite unreliable, depending as it did on the depth of ground at which the remains were found. Now the method of carbon dating is very accurate, even when the evidence is many thousands of years old.
- Techniques for studying the living human brain based on damage from illness and accidents have allowed distinctions to be made among various areas of the brain. For example, it has been known for over a century that the capacity for language is localized in a particular region of the brain (a part of the left frontal lobe).
- The location of functions in the brain has become an increasingly popular area of study since the development of an array of new technologies for imaging which are permitting new discoveries about the live functioning of the human brain.
- Since the discovery of DNA, DNA analysis can be performed on human and animal remains to establish common genetic stock.

5.2 Brain size matters: language and sociality in human evolution

The most significant evolutionary advance in the brains of mammals has been in the increase in size and complexity of the cerebral cortex. Is this the clue, scientists have asked, to the period of evolution when *Homo sapiens* branched off from its ape-like ancestors? Using the kinds of methods mentioned in Box 1.2, it has been established that, over the period that *Homo sapiens* evolved, brain size evolved much faster than in other primate species. This is illustrated in Figure 1.4.

You may be wondering why a focus on brain size is acceptable here when it has been discredited in the study of differences among human groups (see Section 3). The difference is that here scientists are looking at changes in evolutionary time (based on firm evidence), whereas the earlier work was looking for group differences in ability based on differences between the skulls (of recent origin) belonging to various groups of human beings.

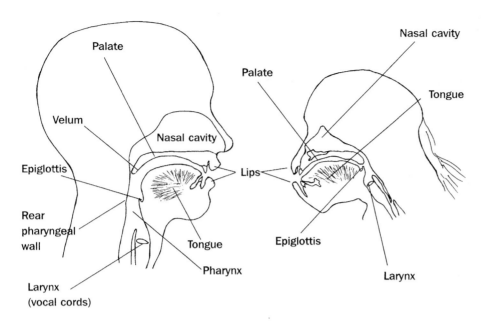

FIGURE 1.4   Comparison of head and neck of a human and a chimpanzee adult

Even four million years ago, for example, human ancestors had larger brains than modern-day chimps (Cartwright, 2000, p.167). The difference, expressed in terms of a ratio, is 1.6 (human brain) to 1.0 (chimpanzee). This did not happen in a smooth growth over time, however: for 1.5 million years, human brain size remained steady and then, over only half a million years, it doubled in size. Because of humans' large brains, babies had to be born earlier and the species would not have survived premature birth had not an appropriate form of social organization of humans into groups also developed, and particularly the caring behaviour of females who gave birth to dependent infants.

It is argued that the period of growth in human brain size corresponded to the development of human language capacity. This fits with the belief that it is humans' language ability that distinguishes them from other animals. It was also thought that brain capacity followed tool use, but evidence from the period when brain size grew so fast does not fit with what appear to be earlier developments in tool use. So what made *Homo sapiens* evolve so fast away from other primate species, coinciding with the growth in brain size? The current theory is that *Homo sapiens*' growth in sociality evolved in parallel with the increase in brain size. In this argument it was the increasingly complex forms of social organization, including the need to ensure survival of premature infants, that precipitated the evolution of human language capacity and the parallel development of specialized areas of the brain. In this recent work, evolutionary science, with its tendency to emphasize the natural, is incorporating the social into its perspectives.

By now you have answers to the question posed in Activity 1.2, 'what distinguishes humans from other animals?' Tool use is important but rudimentary tool use is found in other primates. Sociality is also important but social organization is very strong in other primate species too. Language skills look like the main candidate. Read on.

5.3   Can chimpanzees learn language?

Is language specific to human beings? This question has been pursued by trying to find out whether chimpanzees, as the nearest surviving evolutionary relative to *Homo sapiens*, have language ability. But how was this question to be resolved through scientific study?

ACTIVITY 1.3

Do chimpanzees have language? If you were a scientist (with unlimited resources!) who wanted to answer this question, how would you go about finding out?

Make notes on the following:

- Two possible ways of finding out whether chimpanzees have language.
- The likely strengths and weaknesses of each of these approaches.
- What you would define as evidence of language behaviour in chimpanzees.

For the purposes of this activity, I am not looking for answers of the kind 'I would look on the web', or 'I would use the library' because I want you to think about the strengths and limitations of possible research methods. The reason you need to consider how you would define language is that otherwise you would not know whether the behaviour that you found in chimpanzees demonstrated that they had, or did not have, language. After you have completed the activity, the comment will summarize how this question has been approached by scientists, their mistakes and disagreements.

COMMENT _____

In the 1930s, early psychology experiments literally tried to teach chimpanzees to speak, and it was only later that it was accepted that the failure of these experiments demonstrated not chimps' inability to learn language, but that they did not have the vocal anatomy to make human speech sounds. (You can see how different the anatomy is in Figure 1.4.) Perhaps you, like the American psychologists in the 1930s, equated language with speech. Once this approach was dismissed, what could establish chimps' language ability that did not rely on speech? Sign language is an example of a language that does not rely on the spoken word. Starting in the 1960s, researchers attempted to teach American Sign Language to a chimpanzee called Washoe, who was brought up from the age of one in the family of the researchers. The researchers were trying to mimic the social conditions of growing up in a family that would apply to a human child. For a while it was believed that Washoe was learning language and indeed did learn over a hundred signs. However, this was after thousands of trials, not comparable with a child who, at peak rate, is learning one new word an hour, largely without anyone consciously teaching them. Now the consensus is that Washoe's case did not prove chimps' language ability.

You probably found it difficult to specify what behaviours you would define as coming into the category of language. One of the main problems is to define a decisive set of characteristics that distinguishes language from other kinds of communication. After all, no one denies that animals communicate, both to each other and to humans. Moreover, there are different aspects to language. The Washoe study defined language as the capacity to use signs or symbols. But what about **syntax**? Washoe couldn't manage syntax.

Others argue that, even if a chimp could be taught language in Washoe's way, it would not be relevant to the main question of whether language is a distinctively human ability. This is because chimps have not spontaneously evolved any kind of language (as defined by humans), independent of human intervention. The implication of this argument is that chimps would have to be studied in their natural environment. Indeed, many researchers prefer to study behaviour, whether human or animal, in natural settings. Perhaps in your notes, you imagined yourself setting off for somewhere like the Congo, living in the tropical forests and observing the animals over years.

Recent ethological research in central Africa, which involved observing a colony of gorillas over several years, has discovered that gorillas have a complex system of chest-beating (the sound of which carries quite far, like a drum). Language is usually distinguished from such forms of animal communication by establishing whether it is creative; that is, whether the language user can make up new forms within the structure, or grammar, of the language. Perhaps gorillas can communicate unique events through complex variation of rhythm, speed and volume in their chest-beating. They can enter into a dialogue, not only with each other but also with a human researcher who was using hand clapping to mimic the gorilla's rhythm. This certainly constitutes communication, but whether it is a language depends on how human researchers define the properties of language. This example raises a further problem of method: as humans, how would we really know whether the forms of communication of animals such as these gorillas fulfilled our criteria of language. Perhaps the ultimate experiment would be to reverse the Washoe approach and arrange for a human being to grow up in one of their colonies and learn their 'language'!

Syntax
Syntax is the ability to put symbols into a construction, so that their composition adds up to more than the sum of the individual symbols. For example, 'the wolf killed the baby' and 'the baby killed the wolf', mean different things.

SUMMARY

- Through technological advances in scientific methods, the evolutionary development of *Homo sapiens* has been charted in considerable detail and this knowledge has been applied to the question of human nature.
- Humans and closely related primates are distinctive in their use of tools.
- The larger brain size of humans has been used to explain the language capacity of humans, but brain evolution appears more closely to coincide with the development of human sociality.
- Non-human primates do not have human-like language capacity.

6   HUMAN NATURE ACCORDING TO THE SOCIAL SCIENCES

Writing at around the same time as Darwin, Karl Marx also set out to theorize human nature. He too challenged the religious knowledges that still dominated and he too saw man as a 'natural' being. However, what he emphasized was how a person's natural potentials were actualized in the 'totality of social relations' and how this experience made humans capable of acting in and on their worlds. Marx's emphasis on the totality of social relations making people what they are reflected a broader turn towards the study of social influences on individuals. Human infants are born into social relations and those who study infants agree that they are born with the capacity to relate to others. Here we can see the inseparability of the social and the natural.

Culture

Culture, in its social definition, is 'a description of a particular way of life, which expresses certain meanings and values not only in art and learning but also in institutions and ordinary behaviour' (Williams, 1965, p.57).

Human infants are also born into **culture** and have the capacity to use and reinvent culture. Culture is a concept that was first being developed at the same time as evolutionary theory. One of the first definitions of culture, now famous, is that of Edward Burnett Taylor in 1871 in a book called *Primitive Culture*. He defined culture as 'that complex whole which includes knowledge, belief, art, morals, law, custom and any other capabilities and habits acquired by man as a member of society' (cited in Jahoda, 1992). In other words, culture consists of all the ways in which meanings are attached to practices that would otherwise be habitual and meaningless. See Box 1.3 for observational methods available to study people's cultural activities. Humans can transmit ideas and values from one generation to another. They can represent the meanings that their lives hold for them, for example by stories transmitted through generations, by written language, paintings and cultural practices such as those surrounding burial or adornment. This is referred to as **symbolic capacity**. It is symbolic capacity, rather than language on its own, that distinguishes humans from other animals. Of course language is one hugely significant part of this, but it is not the only way that meanings are made. In the following section the example of death is used in order to develop the idea of symbolic capacity as a defining characteristic of human nature.

Symbolic capacity
The capacity to make and communicate meaning.

BOX 1.3   Observational methods in the social sciences

There are two main ways of studying living people in their natural surroundings. The first is to ask them to provide their own account of whatever the researcher is interested in finding out. This is usually done through an interview. The second way is through observation. This is the most common method for studying human beings in their natural and social settings. There have been many different methods of observation in everyday settings, depending on the object of study. The observational method has a long history, dating back to 1799 when a 'Society of Observers of Man' was founded in Paris. (Its motto was 'Know thyself'.) All observation methods depend on meticulous noticing of behaviours, arrangements and events that might, in everyday life, be taken for granted. What is seen and the sense that is made of it depend, however, on the categories available through which to notice it. For example, looking out of the window, now, I can see a red blob of colour surrounded by green leaves. I know it is a rose. This category enables me to place what I see in the context of all I know about garden flowers and also a whole cultural tradition about the rose; its special smell, its associations with love, the symbolism of its thorns and so on. Social science emphasizes that the knowledge that is produced through observation is mediated by the meanings that the culture of the observer makes available. Broadly, we can divide observational methods into social and psychological.

Social observation

Sociologists and social anthropologists have used observation to study groups of people and their cultural practices. They study culture by gathering evidence of the way people live together in groups and communities. It is possible to study any place where people are living together. Traditionally, social anthropologists sought out people living in remote and unfamiliar cultures because it is difficult, in ones own culture, not to take too much for granted. It is, of course, possible to observe groups closer to home, for example urban gangs. You can categorize methods of social observation based on the amount of participation by the researcher. An example of maximum participation ('going native') is where the researcher joins the group they are studying, for example getting a job as a prison officer or an agency night cleaner. In this case they may not even say that they are doing research so as not to influence the behaviour of those they are studying (this has raised ethical questions). This method is called participant observation. Often observation is combined with interviewing.

Psychological and psychoanalytic observation

Psychologists and psychoanalysts have often used observation to study child development. Darwin and Jean Piaget, an early developmental psychologist, both published studies based on their own children, Darwin on emotional expression and Piaget on the development of reasoning. Children in a special room or nursery can be observed from behind a two-way mirror so that they are not aware of the observer. Psychoanalytic observation has become a formalized method of training for those in the caring professions and particularly for psychotherapists. A family gives permission for visits to the home for one hour at the same time every week for a year. The focus is on observing the infant or child in its social environment. The example in Section 6.3 is taken from an infant observation.

6.1 Death as natural and social

When an archaeologist discovers an ancient burial site and there are artefacts buried with the body (for example, pots, knives, or a brooch), these demonstrate that death is more than a natural fact in the group in which it occurred; it is also a cultural practice. When an animal dies it is abandoned to the forces of nature, its body fed on by predators and decomposed in the course of time. What is it, in contrast, about human nature that means that a living person is motivated to rearrange a corpse and to adorn it? Every human culture ever known has burial practices that invest death with a meaning beyond the natural fact. Figure 1.5 illustrates the burial site of a warrior. An archaeologist who finds a sword and armour beside a corpse in a grave concludes, not only that this person was a warrior, but also that the culture within which he or she lived used the symbols of sword and armour to represent that fact. They also conclude that members of that culture believed in an after-life. An archaeologist will infer that the dead person was furnished with their weapons and armour for an imagined future. In all human cultures people anticipate their own deaths and there are well-established rituals by which the diverse meanings of life and death and morality are enacted when a person dies. The burial practice is part of what shows that humans are aware of their situation in time. Animals are situated in time too (they are born, they die), but they do not know it. The act of burial anticipates a future for the dead person and for those who will remember the burial. It turns the past into history because it records the event of that death through burial.

FIGURE 1.5   The burial site of a warrior

The example of burial indicates a number of aspects of culture. There are those aspects that exist outside a given person, for example cultural practices that are transmitted in language or other forms of representation such as pictorial symbols or burial practices. These are the social aspects of culture. There are also the psychological aspects without which social practices could not have been invented, for example the capacity to imagine the future of a dead person; an imagination that is not built on experience, since no one has ever come back from death. In summary, we can make a distinction between death as an inevitable biological state that is characteristic of both animals and humans and death as a culturally-shared set of meanings that imbues it with significance and demonstrates that it is imagined, remembered and recorded by the living. It is the human capacity for imagination and symbolization that makes culture possible. This is what puts the 'human' in human nature.

6.2 Self-consciousness

The capacity for creating meaning in objects, what above has been called symbolic capacity, is demonstrated by the example of laying significant objects with a corpse. The example of human burial sites suggests a further distinguishing feature of human nature: **self-consciousness**. The living human being who rearranges and adorns the corpse is aware of who she or he is in relation to the dead person: 'I am preparing [my father/my child] for what follows death'. Even if this is not put into words and remains implicit in the actions carried out, it is an inevitable human part of the experience of being in relationship with the dead person. The significance of this act derives from the particular interpersonal relationship that the living person had with the dead person. It also derives from the social structures in which that relationship was located, for example what the duties and expectations are of being a daughter or son in that culture at that point in history. In this way, social relations draw on culture.

Self-consciousness
A person's awareness of himself or herself as if from the perspective of another person.

Relating to someone's death necessarily entails some knowledge, however inarticulate, of being alive. Self-consciousness of being alive implies the awareness of the inevitability of ones own death in the future. These are examples of the capacity for self-consciousness. Three features of self-consciousness illustrated in the burial example are useful to note. The first is how self-consciousness is tied to language (whether spoken or not). Any sentence with 'I' in it is a sign of self-consciousness. The second feature is that self-consciousness arises out of the relationship to the other person. My awareness of myself as alive is in relation to the other being dead, or my awareness of my self as a daughter or mother is a relational term, being significant in relation to the other as my father or child. There are differences of emphasis as to what is the source of this relational ability. Some emphasize language, arguing that it is the grammar that puts us in relation to each other ('I love you'). Others stress human imagination, in particular the emotional capacity to identify with others. Although this is often not conscious, it is enacted in the everyday ways in which we understand ('feel for') the situation another person is in. The third feature is that we are self-conscious as beings in time. The idea of being alive is significant because I understand what death means in terms of my own future, which I can attempt to imagine. These three ideas are developed further below.

The influence of both language and relationships with other people is emphasized in social psychological theories of the self. At the beginning of the twentieth century, C.H. Cooley (1902/1964) coined the idea of a 'looking glass self'. According to Cooley, all human individuals know themselves, not directly, but through using others as the looking glass that reflects themselves back to themselves. G.H. Mead (1934), writing not long after, developed this idea to include the importance of language and its grammar. He argued that the self is divided into the 'I' and the 'me'. The 'I' is the part that does the experiencing and the 'me' is one of the objects experienced (along with you, it, him, her and them). Self-consciousness requires both of these parts; in fact it is achieved through their interaction.

If the self were just a product of a faithful, reflecting mirror of what others saw in one, our experiences in relationships would completely determine who we are. Most psychologists would agree that we are all strongly influenced by the history of our relationships since birth, but would also want to qualify this idea of a social self by saying that we are not determined by others' responses. Explanations of human nature that, like these, have emphasized the social influences on selves often have difficulty when it comes to explaining human agency. The idea of imagination is relevant here. It is not simply how others respond that is important for our experience of our selves, but how we *imagine* that they will respond. Imagination is creative. It goes beyond the facts and can change them too. If we wish for a certain kind of response, which we can imagine, we can also modify our actions to make that more likely. Understanding this capacity to imagine is central to explaining what is distinctly human about human nature.

6.3 Relations with others and the development of symbolic capacity

It seems that newborn babies do not demonstrate self-consciousness, but that this develops gradually in the first few years of life. Some would argue that this capacity is acquired as a result of developing language. Others would emphasize that self-consciousness develops earlier through a baby's relationship to others. A baby's capacity for interpersonal relating is not fully-fledged. The capacities for imagination, for using symbols to make meaning and for putting oneself in the position of the other – all distinctive features of human nature – may be given as capacities at birth but they are only developed through experience.

The following example is taken from a researcher's observation of a baby in her family setting. It illustrates a moment in a baby's experience when a significant relationship and a wish to share something that is pleasurable are converted into the action of pointing. This leads to the construction of a shared meaning and an opportunity for the baby to engage with language and symbolic thought. (See Box 1.3 for further information on this observation method.) Gemma is 11 months and 14 days at the time of the observation.

> Gemma squealed excitedly and pointed at a squirrel just outside the French windows. She turned her head towards her mother, and opened both her mouth and her eyes wide. She then returned her look to the squirrel, maintaining her pointed hand throughout. Her mother came over to the window saying 'Look, you've spotted a squirrel. That's a squirrel there!' Her prosody seemed to match the excitement of her daughter. Gemma responded to this by reinforcing her pointing again. Her mother laughed and said 'Yes I can see, you found a squirrel'. They both appeared to enjoy this, and looked at each other and the squirrel often until the animal disappeared from sight.
>
> (Burhouse, 1999, p.45)

This example illustrates the importance, for the baby, of sharing an interesting experience (one that gives it pleasure) with another person in order to give that experience meaning. Part of the process of giving meaning to the experience is attaching a positive significance to it through the other person's response. The mother in this extract takes the position of her baby, in the sense that she empathizes with her excitement and echoes it back. The extract nicely demonstrates that Gemma is not a passive recipient of what is happening outside in her environment. Rather she demonstrates active agency, both in her emotional response to the sight of the squirrel and by including her mother in the experience. She probably knows that her excited squeals will attract her mother's attention, and by pointing at the squirrel with her hand, she directs her mother's attention to the object of her interest. In the following turns of their interaction, Gemma will begin to build meaning, and the beginnings of language ('that's a squirrel, there') onto her sensory and emotional experience. The connection is a three-way one: between Gemma, her mother and the object of their joint attention, the squirrel. Developmental psychologists emphasizing the importance of **intersubjectivity** believe that it is within this three-way space that human symbolic capacity is developed.

Intersubjectivity
The dynamics that flow between two people's experiencing.

6.4   Imagination and being-in-time

The capacity for imagination is an extraordinarily powerful one because it adds the possibility of creativity to human experience of the environment. In a person's imagination symbols do not obediently just stand in for the objects they represent, rather they can take on an extra life because the imagination does not have to be constrained by reality. Remember the burial example: the idea that a dead warrior will need their sword and shield in a future life is a creative imagining that goes beyond reality. Art, science, technology and religion are only possible because human imaginings have exceeded the existing experience of those involved.

Imagination only achieves these cultural products when put into practice over extended periods of time. Humans are aware of living in time. In other words, we have knowledge of a past and a future to our lives as well as a present. This means that, unlike in animals, human actions can be suspended and deferred in order to pursue complex goals. Imagination combined with awareness of being-in-time breaks the immediate connection between a need and the performance of an action that attempts to meet that need. A need can be postponed by holding an idea in the mind over time even in the absence of the actual object or person that is represented. In this view, imagination undermines the dominance of instinct over behaviour; it transforms the force of animal nature in human behaviour.

Often human nature is reduced to the idea of instincts, as if these determine behaviour directly and in a way that evades intention and control. Now we can see how instincts do not get direct expression in human behaviour because of humans' unique symbolic capacities: for thought, imagination and self-consciousness.

SUMMARY

- While natural science has charted the developing capacities of humans over evolutionary time, social science has focused on the expression of human capacities through social relations and culture in their accounts of human nature.

- Social and psychological observation methods provide information about people in their everyday social context.

- Archaeological study of burial sites suggests that, unlike with animals, death is treated symbolically in all human cultures.

- The creation and use of symbols is seen as a defining feature of human nature.

- Self-consciousness is also seen as a feature of human nature. It is understood as a capacity that develops in relationships, both in their real and imaginary aspects, as a result of the capacity to symbolize.

- Humans, unlike other animals, are aware of their existence in time, aware of their past and their future. Combined with the human capacity for imagining what is outside their experience, humans can be creative in making and changing things. In other words, they can be agents. This too is a distinctive feature of human nature.

7 SEX AND HUMAN NATURE

Of all human activities, sex is seen as the most natural. In this section, I question this bit of common sense. First I want you to explore your own assumptions about sex as a natural and social act. The first part of this section then acts as a commentary and critique of the idea of sex as a natural activity. The second part builds the argument for sex as a symbolic activity.

ACTIVITY 1.4

- Give two reasons why sex can be thought of as primarily a natural human behaviour.

- Next, give two reasons why it can be thought of as primarily social.

You will find my answers to these questions woven into the following text. Look out for them and see how closely they resemble yours.

7.1 Accounts of human sex as a natural act

People tend to believe that sex is a prime example of a natural human activity because if it were not for sex (they are thinking only of heterosexual intercourse in this context) the human species would not get reproduced and would not survive. This is an example of the way that evolutionary theory has permeated ordinary understanding of what is natural. Evolutionary theory tells us that adaptations get selected if they help a species survive and this selection happens through genetic mechanisms passed on through generations via sexual reproduction. It must be the case, then, that there are some natural features laid down in human heredity that enable humans to have sexual intercourse. What are these natural features? First, as is commonly done, we can look to animal sexual behaviour to see if comparisons can be drawn as to what is natural in humans.

According to scientific evidence, in non-human primates and many other mammalian species, females have oestrus; that is, they have cycles of sexual receptivity (for example, female dogs go 'on heat'). During oestrus, certain chemicals are manufactured that send signals to males in whom a sexual response is triggered. This is how, in many species, sexual reproduction is ensured. The significant point to make about this sexual instinct in animal species is that the signal and the response are not self-conscious or intentional or known about by the individuals that participate. (This is one reason why the use of terms like 'rape' or 'courtship' applied to animal behaviour is so misleading.) Biologists point out that human females do not have chemically determined cycles of sexual availability and unavailability and therefore human males' sexual arousal is not triggered by such chemical signals. But how is the significance of the scientific evidence to be interpreted? It is likely that human sexual practices are not triggered in this direct, automatic manner because they have entered the symbolic realm, which mediates the experience of bodily sensations by the meanings that are made of them.

Another approach to looking for natural features is to look to specifically human biology. Human reproductive biology (genital anatomy and hormone differences) is specialized in males and females, given genetically through the XY and XX sex chromosomes respectively (the X and Y refer to their appearance when looked at under a microscope). This much is accepted as fact (although not all individuals are clearly one sex or the other). Human males and females are sexually differentiated and have anatomical and hormonal capacities that make their parts in reproduction necessarily different. This, however, explains little about the *use* of the body's reproductive capacity. The only kind of sexual behaviour that results in human reproduction is heterosexual penis–vagina intercourse resulting in male ejaculation at a fertile time in the female's menstrual cycle (this is the mode of sexual intercourse that mammals engage in). This does not account for most of human sexual activity. The argument that sex is natural because it ensures the reproduction of the species fails to explain all the ways in which human sexual activity does not lead to reproduction.

ACTIVITY 1.5 (PART ONE)

Make a list of four types of human sexual activity that do not lead to reproduction.

COMMENT

Was homosexual sex on your list of human sexual activities that do not lead to reproduction? It was on mine. However, so were the following, which refer to heterosexual sex: heterosexual intercourse using contraception, non-penetrative sex, sex at the non-fertile time of the menstrual cycle. When it is claimed that homosexual sex is 'unnatural', this claim relies on the idea that nature dictates only sexual behaviour that leads to the reproduction of the species, namely heterosexual intercourse. Clearly many human sexual activities do not lead to reproduction.

7.2 An account of human sex as a social act

Let us then look briefly at a social account of sexuality and sexual preference. I will focus on the example of homosexuality. Children are born into a pre-existing cultural environment. This includes sets of meanings about homosexuality that will vary across time and place. Michel Foucault (1979) has argued, using historical evidence from Western culture, that for hundreds of years homosexual practices coexisted with heterosexual ones, without those involved incurring a label as homosexual (or for that matter as heterosexual). It was relatively recently in European cultures, during the nineteenth century, that the label 'homosexual' was applied to the person, producing an identity for individuals and groups where previously there had been a diversity of sexual practices. Through this new way of knowing, meanings were generated that created heterosexuality as a norm against which homosexuals deviated and could be punished. Such a way of knowing also created the conditions for resistance, so that now groups of homosexuals have produced alternative ways of knowing, cultural practices and social relations. These provide individuals with ways of making sense of sexual feelings and experiences and also forms of social relations that afford wider opportunities for expressing sexuality in relation to others. In other words, new labels are provided through cultural changes and these can be attached to sexual practices.

7.3 A psychoanalytic account of human sex as a psycho-social act

The above description emphasizes how social relations and culture shape the way in which homosexuality (and heterosexuality) can be expressed and provide the context in which people can make sense of their sexuality. However, the availability of a set of cultural practices and ways of knowing about homosexuality do not create homosexuals (although politicians sometimes act as if they do). The explanation requires supplementing to make it **psycho-social**. If at the same time we introduce a psychoanalytic perspective, it can help to account for how different people experience their sexual feelings and attractions and how these can feel outside their conscious control. (These feelings are often assumed to be biological, as if only something natural could be so strongly felt.)

Freud argued that the infant is bisexual because it does not recognize such a thing as the sex or gender of its initial carer, but derives pleasure and wants attention irrespective of whether the person concerned is a woman or a man, same sex or other sex. If all human babies are born bisexual then it is necessary to explain how, as adults, people become hetero- or homo- or bi-sexual. Freud used case studies to show that human sexual attraction is specific to the meanings conjured up in the imagined or actual relationship

Psycho-social
Psycho-social refers to an explanation of behaviour that takes into account the interconnections of social and psychological factors – and hopefully biological ones too. Recent uses of the term draw on psychoanalysis because it pays useful attention to the development of a person over their life course and to unconscious processes and to intersubjectivity.

with the other person. These meanings carry unconscious traces of desire for one or both of the parents. In this view heterosexuality requires as much explanation as any other sexuality: it cannot be assumed to be 'natural' and therefore in need of no other explanation.

Freud claimed that the sexual instinct was the driving principle in human nature. However, he was not talking about a sexual instinct that would compel a human being to have sexual intercourse. Rather he was defining sex in a way that drew inspiration from understanding the pleasures experienced by newborn babies. For Freud, babies' sexual pleasure was not something that resided in the genitals, rather sexual pleasure spread over the surface of the whole body especially in response to touch. The infant's most sensitive area for this pleasure is the mouth. This makes sense because sucking is the means of the infant feeding itself and without experiencing pleasure it would not be motivated to do so and would not thrive. However, the pleasure of sucking is a lot more than a natural oral instinct. The infant, when it is having a satisfying feed at the breast, is held in secure arms and hears the familiar heartbeat (one of the few continuities of experience from foetal life). It is suffused by warmth, surrounded by familiar body smell and can feel the contact of skin on the skin of another at the breast.

FIGURE 1.6

This experience is natural in that it involves all the senses, and it is psychological in the sense that it is the foundation of that individual's experience of feeling secure in the world. The experience is also social in that it is tied to dependence on another person, not just for physical care, but for psychological dependability. Building trust in early relationships is just one element that will affect later, sexual relationships. From such early experiences all later bodily pleasures derive part of their meaning, according to Freud, including the later pleasures of sex, which are not confined to the genitals, but also encompass the whole body. The early foundations on which later sexual pleasure is built are thus relational and symbolic as well as sensual.

ACTIVITY 1.5 (PART TWO)

When you completed the first part of Activity 1.5, perhaps you were defining sexual activity quite narrowly in terms of genital activity. Now add four more types of sexual activity that do not lead to reproduction drawing on Freud's broader definitions above.

COMMENT _____

The following is one example of the two lists of types of human sexual activity that do not lead to reproduction (with an extra item on each for good measure):

- homosexual sex, masturbation, heterosexual intercourse using contraception, non-penetrative sex, sex at the non-fertile time of the menstrual cycle
- kissing, dancing, undressing, stroking, sex with fetish objects.

You might be wondering what makes activities such as undressing (sometimes) sexual. Undressing in particular contexts achieves a symbolic status whose meanings are linked to past occasions and past representations of sexual relating and perhaps imagined and wished for future ones. This is what renders them sexual.

_____

These arguments do not mean that biological mechanisms are irrelevant in human sexual behaviour, only that these will be overlaid by meanings provided by a combination of psychological and social circumstances past, present and imagined future. For example, cultural practices concerning sexuality do not cancel out the fact that there is the greatest concentration of nerve endings anywhere in the body located in the human female clitoris, and, slightly less so, in the human male penis. This neural sensitivity is not an evolutionary accident; rather it enables a plenitude of sensations that, under the right conditions, are enormously pleasurable. However, the nerve endings do not guarantee pleasure (they can also be the means for the experience of pain) and, given human symbolic capacity and the relational nature of the self, the right conditions will entail a consideration of the meanings of that sexual activity. Many women in many different cultures have gone through life not experiencing any sexual pleasure, and not knowing that any was possible or how to produce it.

SUMMARY

- Sex has commonly been seen as a typically natural act, because it is necessary for human reproduction and because it is often experienced as driven or instinctual.

- Most sexual practices do not lead to reproduction and so the idea that sex is natural because it leads to reproduction is inadequate.

- For the same reason, heterosexuality and homosexuality should not logically be thought of as respectively 'natural' and 'unnatural'.

- The idea of a homosexual is of quite recent historical origin and this has influenced how people experience and put into practice same-sex desires.

- The example of a baby's early sensual and sexual experience and its psychological significance in later life showed how sex can be understood as both natural and social at the same time once psychological experience is also incorporated.

- Experience, for example of sex, relies on a lifetime of meanings that are drawn from culture and social relations and transformed through imagination, needing and symbolization to make them creative and not determined by social structures.

8 CONCLUSION

The idea of human nature has, over a long history, been caught up in justifying how powerful groups treat other groups. For centuries the understanding of human nature has been limited by the dualistic thought contained in the terms natural and social. In this chapter I have identified several distinctive features of human nature that all interact together.

- Humans symbolize; that is, they have symbolic capacity, communicate with each other through symbols and use symbols to create and understand culture.

- Humans have self-consciousness, developed and enacted through interpersonal and social relations.

- Humans are aware of being-in-time. This both enables symbolization and is enabled by it.

- Humans have imaginative capacity that enables creativity in making things, making culture and relating to people. It explains why people are agents in their lives, more than the sum of external (social and physical) and internal (biological) structures that impinge upon them.

- The capacities for these human characteristics must derive from nature (more specifically, genes, hormones, bodily structures and the like), but it is in the social environment, mediated by human psychology, that human nature is expressed.

REFERENCES

Burhouse, A. (1999) 'Me, you and it: conversations about the significance of joint attention skills from cognitive psychology, child development research and psychoanalysis', unpublished MA Dissertation in Psychoanalytic Observation Studies, Tavistock Clinic and University of East London.

Cartwright, J. (2000) *Evolution and Human Behaviour: Darwinian Perspectives on Human Nature*, London, Macmillan.

Cooley, C.H. (1902/1964) *Human Nature and the Social Order*, New York, Schocken Books.

Darwin, C. (1859) *On the Origin of Species by Means of Natural Selection*, London, John Murray.

Foucault, M. (1979) *The History of Sexuality, Volume One, An Introduction*, London, Allen Lane.

Freud, S. (1920/1955) *Beyond the Pleasure Principle*, standard edition vol.18, London, Hogarth.

Freud, S. (1930/1961) *Civilization and Its Discontents*, standard edition vol.21, London, Hogarth.

Goldblatt, D. (ed.) (2004) *Knowledge and the Social Sciences: Theory, Method, Practice* (2nd edn), London, Routledge/The Open University.

Jahoda, G. (1992) *Crossroads between Culture and Mind: Continuities and Change in Theories of Human Nature*, London, Harvester Wheatsheaf.

Mead, G.H. (1934) *Mind, Self and Society*, Chicago, University of Chicago Press.

Thompson, K. and Woodward, K. (2004) 'Knowing and believing: religious knowledge' in Goldblatt, D. (ed.).

Williams, R. (1965) *The Long Revolution*, Harmondsworth, Penguin.

Woodward, K. and Watt, S. (2004) 'Science and society: knowledge in medicine' in Goldblatt, D. (ed.).

FURTHER READING

Ashworth, P. (2000) *Psychology and 'Human Nature'*, Hove, Taylor and Francis. This approachable book looks at various psychological theories of human nature.

Cartwright, J. (2000) *Evolution and Human Behaviour: Darwinian Perspectives on Human Nature*, London, Macmillan. If you want to know a great deal about evolutionary theory, this is a biologist's detailed and scholarly account.

Jahoda, G. (1992) *Crossroads between Culture and Mind: Continuities and Change in Theories of Human Nature*, London, Harvester Wheatsheaf. This is a unique historical account of developments in thinking about culture and mind in Europe. It is full of intriguing details and flashes of insight.

Stevenson, L. (1974/1987) *Seven Theories of Human Nature*, Oxford, Oxford University Press. This includes accessible overviews of some diverse approaches to human nature: Christianity, Freud, Lorenz, Marx, Sartre, Skinner and Plato.

Stevenson, L. (ed.) (1981) *The Study of Human Nature, Readings*, Oxford, Oxford University Press. This consists of edited readings from many philosophers and scientists and includes approaches outside the Western tradition.

Whose health is it anyway?

Brenda Smith and David Goldblatt

Contents

1 INTRODUCTION

In Chapter 1 of this book Wendy Hollway discussed the way in which our *natural* biological make-up interacts with the kind of *social* circumstances in which we live in different areas of human experience and at different times. We saw that there are complex interactions between what society provides and what we can do ourselves as agents.

As one of the authors of this chapter, and as an asthma sufferer, I am only too aware of how my biology interacts with my social and physical environment so that I avoid certain activities and certain places. However, despite taking care, I sometimes get a full-blown attack and this affects my ability to take part in my normal everyday activities. So it is of key interest to me what causes asthma and what might be the best way for me to deal with its effects. Is it primarily a biological condition that I can only hope to control with drugs? Is it a condition brought on by the urban environment in which I live? Is it exacerbated by the fact that I smoke? Controlling my asthma requires constant medication, so my 'illness' has a cost on the health service. Therefore, dealing with my asthma and that of other sufferers is of interest not just to me, but also to the government and indeed to everyone who pays for and utilizes the health service. So, looking at the causes of health and illness and possible interventions offers another way in which we can explore how the natural interacts with the social conditions in which we live.

Health seems to play an increasing role in our everyday lives. It is difficult to pick up a newspaper or magazine, listen to the television or radio, or visit a bookshop without being confronted with information on health or exhortations to avoid certain foods, take certain vitamins or minerals, take regular exercise and a host of other things. It seems that everyone is concerned with health – not just doctors and health care professionals, but the government, the media and indeed all of us who each year make resolutions to eat more healthily, drink or smoke less and take regular exercise. A lot of this information and advice seems to suggest that we can influence the extent to which we enjoy good health through the food we eat, the exercise we take (or don't take), the 'good' or 'bad' habits we have. In other words, we each seem to be responsible for whether or not we enjoy full, active, healthy lives.

Make a note of the sources of information and advice on health that you have come across. Which ones do you take particular note of?

Think about what you do to take care of your health.

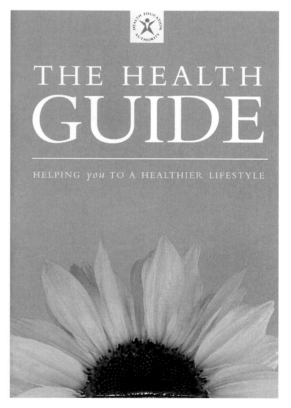

FIGURE 2.1   The official line: government advice on the healthy life

However, despite this rhetoric of responsibility for oneself and one's health, a close look at the same sources tells us that atmospheric pollution is a major problem of the era and that it is largely responsible for breathing difficulties such as asthma in our cities. In the twenty-first century we are also witnessing widespread concerns about the health effects of genetically-engineered food and heated debates about just how 'natural' the fruit and vegetables in our shops and supermarkets are. Increasingly, too, we hear about the medical discoveries of genes which play a part in the development of diseases such as cancer, whilst drug companies constantly seem to produce new treatments for many forms of disease. Many sources also suggest that feelings of being uneasy with ourselves and the stresses and strains of everyday life cause many illnesses. These arguments seem to suggest that there are many causes of illness which are not within the individual's control.

FIGURE 2.2   Take a deep breath – the pleasures of the motor car?

So, who or what is responsible for our health? Is it a matter of luck as to the kind of body we happen to have been born with? Is it to do with our lifestyle, our social or physical environment or the technology typical of Western industrialized societies? These are important questions. As individuals we are concerned to maximize our own health. However, these issues are also important for society as a whole. Apart from moral reasons for maximizing the health of the nation, provision of health services places a considerable financial burden on taxpayers. In Britain, around 7 per cent of the Gross Domestic Product (an indicator of the nation's income) is spent on health care services, whilst working time lost through illness places pressure on business and other organizations.

Most of us when we are ill consult a doctor. In the UK, each of us is entitled to register with a general practitioner who, if it is felt appropriate, can refer us on to a specialist or a hospital. This network of health services, paid for by taxpayers, but free at the point of usage, was set up in 1948 with the establishment of the National Health Service in the UK, which replaced a patchwork of private, co-operative and charitable arrangements. At that time, there was considerable optimism that free access to medical services would transform the health of the nation and clearly there have been considerable successes; life expectancies have increased, neonatal death rates and deaths from childhood illnesses have fallen. However, since the 1970s there has been increasing uncertainty about the power, by themselves, of medicine and conventional doctor- and hospital-based health services to maximize health.

This chapter traces the history of the growth of this uncertainty about how we should seek to improve the health of people in Western industrialized societies. In particular, we will examine how different conceptions of health and illness lead to different ways of seeking to maximize health; and how different forms of evidence have encouraged a more diverse explanation of how to improve health. During our historical tour we shall see how some explanations place emphasis on the role of structural features of our bodies or society whilst others are more concerned with the role that individuals play in making healthy choices.

The primary concern of this chapter is of course to examine how natural and social factors impact upon our health. Clearly, biological factors are important since none of us is born with a perfect body. The influence of biology in relation to health is most clearly stated in medical views of health and illness, so it is with an examination of just how medicine understands health and illness and how it conceives of the best method of treatment that we will begin.

SUMMARY

Working on this chapter will help you to:

- understand and give examples of different conceptions of health and illness;

- understand and describe the growth of uncertainty about how to maximize health and give examples of the more diverse approaches that have been proposed;

- understand how natural and social factors interact in health and illness;

- understand and give examples of the interaction of structural features and individual choice in health and illness.

2 'NATURAL' EXPLANATIONS: MEDICAL CONCEPTIONS OF HEALTH AND ILLNESS

For many of us, ideas about health and illness are largely derived from orthodox Western medicine. In contemporary UK society, doctors are seen as *experts*. They advise us on how to avoid certain illnesses, diagnose us when we are ill, and devise and deliver the best treatment. To many of us this way of thinking about health and illness is 'natural', in other words, it isn't usually open to argument. But, beliefs about what health and illness are and what makes us ill have changed over time and are different across the globe, and indeed, as we shall see, vary between different groups in UK society. Thus, health and disease are what social scientists call **contested concepts**.

What this means is that there is no one 'right' way of understanding health and illness. Now this does not mean that any explanation will do or that they are all accorded equal status. Rather, it suggests that we need to understand the different origins, language and logic of different health beliefs and examine the evidence which supports their claims and concerns.

Medical explanations of health and illness are based on particular views about:

- the relation between our bodies and our minds;
- what health and illness are;
- what makes for effective understanding.

2.1 The relation between the body and the mind: notions of health and illness

Until the seventeenth century, the soul and the body were seen as inextricably linked. Thus, conceptions of life and death, health and illness could not be separated from considerations of faith, sin and salvation. However, in the seventeenth century the philosopher René Descartes (1596–1650) challenged this view. He proposed that there were two kinds of what he called 'substances' in the world. The first is the mind, and the second is matter. In his view, mind is purely consciousness and doesn't take up space in the world, whilst matter (e.g. the body) does take up room in space. Thus, mind and body are subject to different forces. Spiritual forces act on the mind, but these are quite separate from the physical forces which operate on the body. This separation, or **dualism** as it became known, made it possible to understand the human body quite separately from spiritual or religious concerns. Furthermore, while only humans have matter *and* minds (Descartes

Contested concepts
Ideas over which there is basic disagreement, where meanings are not stable and where there may be social differences, debates and conflict.

Dualism
An understanding which suggests that one idea or process is defined in relation to what it is not. A system of understanding based on opposites.

viewed other living things as consisting purely of matter), our bodies are nevertheless subject to the same physical forces which operate on the bodies of other living creatures and can be expected to work in a similar way.

Alongside these philosophical changes there were many important medical advances, especially during the nineteenth and twentieth centuries. For example, there were technical advances such as the stethoscope that marked a change in the way doctors interacted with their patients. Prior to this, doctors had to rely very much on what patients reported and what they felt was wrong. The stethoscope allowed doctors to 'see inside' the patient and make their own observations of the body without having to rely on what the patient said or on outward signs of illness such as coughing. Pioneering laboratory experiments by people such as Pasteur found that some illnesses were due to micro-organisms entering the body. Together, these advances encouraged a view of illness as located within the biology of the body, with distinct causes which could be

FIGURE 2.3   René Descartes (1596–1650) (engraving by W. Holl, after a portrait by Frans Hals)

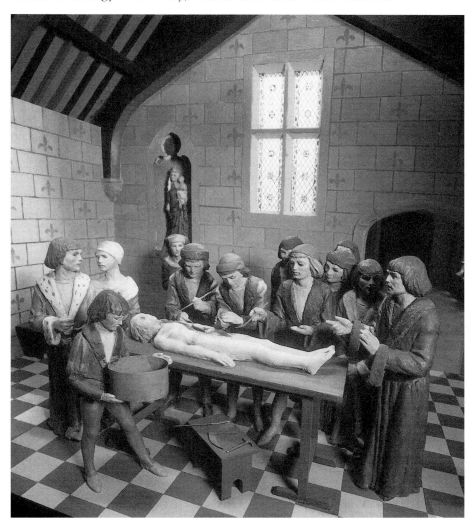

FIGURE 2.4   A sixteenth-century anatomical dissection in Fabricus's anatomical theatre, Padua, Italy

discovered by the doctor without the patient's help. Combined with the philosophical separation of the body and the mind, the way was cleared for doctors to see the study of the body as part of 'nature', subject to the same kinds of forces as other animals and amenable to study in similar ways. This mind and body dualism is analogous to, and works in tandem with, the separation of society and nature as pure opposites (see the Introduction to this book).

Descartes' view of the body was that it was essentially like a machine. Good machines tend to have many component parts working in concert to perform particular tasks. So, the ideal 'body' became linked with the idea of a well-oiled machine in which all the parts work together in harmony. When machines are working well or 'normally', we don't tend intervene. Only when they break down do we send for the mechanic or service engineer. So too doctors tended to be less interested in our bodies when they were working normally and usually only became involved when they 'broke down' or worked 'abnormally'. Over the years, doctors have sought to identify the causes of our 'machine' breaking down and to find ways of 'fixing' it. You will not be greatly surprised then to discover that doctors frequently have some difficulty in defining health and tend to define it in negative terms as the absence of disease. The machine analogy also excludes the idea of agency and subjective experience. Machines are not able to be involved in, or to take responsibility for, their own malfunctioning.

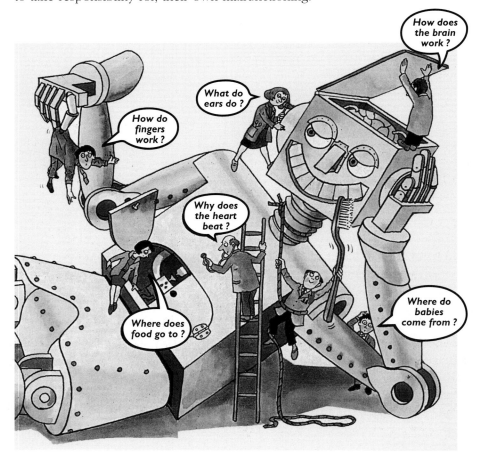

FIGURE 2.5
The body as a machine:
a contemporary image
from a children's
reference book

2.2 Effective understanding

The conception of illness as due to biological forces, and the ability to diagnose illness without the involvement or influence of the patient, gradually encouraged medicine to take on board the methods of the natural sciences which were transforming other aspects of our world in the eighteenth and nineteenth centuries.

Scientific methods are characterized by the systematic study of events. Complex entities like the body are broken down into manageable parts such as organs that can be observed and measured by the physical senses. Since particular organs such as the heart serve the same function in everyone's body, then in principle all hearts operate in the same way, so it doesn't matter who makes the measurements. Furthermore, hearts are assumed not to influence or be influenced by the act of observation. These assumptions have important implications. Firstly, they allow measurements to be independent: in principle everyone who uses a particular kind of measurement will come up with the same answer. Secondly, they allow doctors to build up understanding of the parts and to discern regularities and patterns in illness which can be expressed as law-like universal statements. Medicine thus came to see itself and be seen by others as the accumulation of 'facts'. The strength of such understanding lies in the notion that the observations are not affected by the observer – they are said to be objective, and so they can be reproduced time after time allowing us to be pretty sure of our findings. It is this which has helped scientific medicine to become the most prominent way of understanding health and illness in our society. Indeed, it is often contrasted with other ways of understanding especially in dualistic thinking which presents only two possibilities: good science and bad science or science and superstition. For example, the British Medical Association describes it thus: 'In as much as scientific medicine lays such a firm emphasis on observation, measurement and reproducibility, historically it has become inevitably and increasingly separated from doctrines embracing superstition, magic and the supernatural' (BMA, 1986, p.61).

The many medical advances of the twentieth century provide ample evidence for the success of the medical model. Through the understanding of the microbiological processes of the body and how it fights disease, vaccination programmes such as that for polio have more or less eliminated the disease in Europe and North America. The scientific method has also allowed individual doctors to combine their knowledge with pharmacologists and chemists and so produce important treatments for common diseases. For example, heart attack is one of the most common causes of death in Europe. Over the years, individual doctors utilized a variety of drugs and treatments to help minimize the effect of the attack and to prevent death. However, because of this diversity in treatment, nobody really knew which was best. In the 1980s, a group of doctors in Oxford organized an international study to compare two of the most popular drugs. By looking into the body, it had been discovered that heart attacks are caused by blood clots getting stuck in the arteries of the heart. Blood cannot get through the arteries and a heart attack ensues. Chemical analysis of a particular chemical compound demonstrated its action of effectively 'thinning' the blood. Thus, giving this compound to someone having a heart attack was hypothesized to help get the blood flowing around the heart again, thereby reducing damage. Patients entering hospital with a heart attack were randomly allocated to either drug A or drug B and their progress was monitored. The results revealed that the patients on drug A were very much more likely to survive. The results of this study were published and, within a few years, the drug was used by almost every doctor in Europe and North America and had substantially reduced the number of deaths due to heart attack. The name of drug A was aspirin.

It was these positive effects of widespread application of the medical model of health that created much optimism in the middle of the twentieth century. The establishment of the National Health Service had resulted in people no longer being required to pay doctors directly, so it was thought that this would permit health to become a reality for everyone in society, not just the well off.

From the description above we can see that medicine has a very clear view on 'nature'. Traditionally, for doctors, health is intimately related to our biological nature. Whilst aspects of our biology are specific to our species, it is nevertheless understood that biological processes operate in a very similar way in both human and non-human animals. We can best understand how our biological 'nature' operates in health and illness by adopting the same kind of method that scientists studying non-human animals employ. This scientific method has considerable power to aid our understanding of not just the causes of illness, but also of how illnesses should be treated.

It is also clear that doctors place more emphasis on structural factors than individual choice in their explanations of health and illness. Doctors do not completely reject the impact of individual choice; for example, they exhort us to stop smoking, to reduce our fat intake and to drink in moderation. However, when it comes to understanding the causes of health and illness and how best to organize treatment, they emphasize the biological *structure* of the body. The health choices we make in our everyday lives are of importance for our health only insofar as they affect that biological structure.

SUMMARY

According to the medical explanation of health and illness:

- the mind is separate from the body;
- the body is like a complex 'machine';
- illness is located in the biology of the body;
- knowledge and understanding are achieved through scientific investigation.

3 SOCIAL EXPLANATIONS: THE IMPACT OF SOCIAL CLASS

The dominance of medical views of health and illness was enshrined in the structure and practice of the National Health Service. There was considerable confidence that an objective medical profession would harness the power of modern science and technology to cure many if not most of the common illnesses and, as we noted in Section 2, there were many successes. Furthermore, since access to medical services would be determined by need rather than ability to pay, it was hoped that the overall health of the nation would improve. A service that was free at the point of delivery, would, it was hoped, eliminate the disadvantages of social divisions, especially of social class.

However, considerable blows to this optimism occurred with the publication of two important government reports – 'The Black Report' in 1980 and 'The health divide' in 1992. The groups who produced these reports collected and analysed information about the relationship between social class and health. They looked at various statistics that purport to monitor the state of the nation's health. These include mortality (death rates), morbidity (illness rates) and life expectancy statistics.

Infant mortality is often taken as an indicator of the state of a nation's health. This is often expressed in terms of the infant mortality rate which is the number of babies who die per 1,000 live births. During the second half of the twentieth century, there appeared to have been considerable success in reducing infant mortality in Britain. In 1950, there were 31 infant deaths for every 1,000 live births, but by 1980 this figure dropped to 12, in 1990 the figure was only 8 (*Social Trends*, 1992) and in 2000, the figure was 5.4 (*Social Trends*, 2002). This seems to suggest a downward trend and that overall the National Health Service has had a profound effect and its hopes of reducing 'needless' deaths are being fulfilled. However, a closer look at the figures indicates that babies who die are not randomly spread across all groups in society. Rather, analysis of the figures suggests that certain babies are more at risk. The following table is based on work presented by Carey Oppenheim and Lisa Harker, who use evidence of the experience of poverty to demonstrate the links between social class and morbidity and early mortality.

ACTIVITY 2.1

Look at Table 2.1 overleaf which compares infant mortality in 1978–79 with 1992 in relation to social class.

1   How did infant and perinatal mortality change between 1978 and 1992?
2   Given the general trend, what are the differences between the social classes?

Social class is defined by the Registrar-General for England and Wales in the following way:

I   Professional (for example lawyer, doctor, accountant)

II   Intermediate (for example teacher, nurse, manager)

IIIN Skilled non-manual (for example typist, shop assistant)

IIIM Skilled manual (for example miner, bus driver, cook)

IV   Partly skilled manual (for example farm worker, bus conductor)

V   Unskilled manual (for example cleaner, labourer)

Other Armed forces and economically inactive

TABLE 2.1   Perinatal and infant mortality rates per 1,000 total births 1978–79 and 1992 compared by social class (for marriage births only)

	Perinatal		Infant	
Social class	1978–79	1992	1978–79	1992
I	11.9	6.3	9.8	5.0
II	12.3	6.1	10.1	4.6
III (non-manual)	13.9	6.8	11.1	5.5
III (manual)	15.1	7.0	12.4	5.6
IV	16.7	7.4	13.6	5.8
V	20.3	8.9	17.2	7.9
Other	20.4	10.2	23.3	10.5
Ratio of social class V:I	1.71	1.4	1.8	1.6

Note: Perinatal deaths are those occurring during the first 28 days, infant deaths are those occurring between 28 days and 1 year.
Source: Oppenheim and Harker, 1996, Table 4.2, p.79

C O M M E N T

By looking across the *rows* in the table we can compare the rates for 1978–79 and 1992 in each social class. Thus, for example, we can see that for social class I the rate of perinatal death declined from 11.9 to 6.3, and the rate of infant death from 9.8 to 5.0. If you look at each row you will see that this reduction is repeated in every case. We can therefore say that this table shows a reduction in all deaths of babies during the period between 1978–79 and 1992.

However, if we now look at the *columns* in the table, we can see that in 1978–79 the rate of perinatal deaths showed an increase across the social classes from 11.9 in social class I to 20.3 in social class V. If you look at each column you will see that this story or 'trend' is repeated for both 1978–79 and 1992. Thus, children born to parents in social class V appear to be at more risk of dying than do the children born to parents in social class I.

Other analyses show that deaths are highest for babies whose mothers are under 16 or over 35. The majority of babies who die during the first year are also those who have a low birth-weight. Low birth-weight is associated with mothers who are less well off and may be linked to other factors. Low birth-weight is also associated with smoking tobacco which is also an important component of differences in mortality between social classes. The proportion of smokers is higher among those in the manual socio-economic groups for both men and women than among those in the non-manual groups. The proportion of people who smoke has fallen in Great Britain since the 1970s, although this decline has been greater for some groups than others. In 1972, a third of both men and women in the professional social class were smokers but by 1998–99 this had reduced by more than a half (*Social Trends*, 2002).

There are large variations in infant mortality rates in the United Kingdom by social class. For babies born inside marriage in 1997, the infant mortality rate for those whose fathers were unskilled was one and a half times higher than that for those whose fathers were in the professional social class. For babies born outside of marriage, the mortality rate was 6.9 deaths per thousand live births compared with 5.2 deaths per thousand live births for those born inside marriage. There have, however, been large increases in the proportions of babies born outside marriage for all social classes. Many of these births are jointly registered, reflecting the increase in cohabitation. Although infant mortality rates in each class have decreased over the last decade or so, there is no evidence that the class differential has decreased over this period (*Social Trends*, 2002). So, it would seem that babies of young mothers who are poor are starting off life with a disadvantage. Even more sadly, the disadvantage of being born into the lower social classes seems to continue throughout the life course.

Although life expectancy at birth has increased over the past 30 years among all social classes, there remain inequalities. Given current mortality rates, males born in 1997–99 in England and Wales to parents in the professional group could expect to live, if they remained in that social class, to the age of 78.5 years. This was over 7 years longer than males born to parents in the unskilled manual group. Between 1972–76 and 1992–96 the gap between these social classes widened from 5.5 years to 9.5 years. The gap between these two groups then narrowed again to 7.4 years in 1997–99. There was a similar difference across the social classes for females, with those born to parents in the professional group in 1997–99 having a life expectancy 5.7 years longer than those born to parents in the unskilled manual group.

In the 30 years following the establishment of the NHS mortality rates for adults in social classes IV and V remained the same but there was a marked improvement in mortality rates for people in social classes I and II. Indeed, there is a clear and persistent social gradient in mortality rates at all ages. Of the 66 major causes of death, 62 are more prevalent in social classes IV and V than in other social classes. Rather than diminishing, it appears that class differences in health chances are increasing. Whitehead summed up these findings in 'The health divide' by saying that 'diseases of affluence have all but disappeared and what is left is a general health disadvantage of the poor' (Whitehead, 1992, p.232).

As Oppenheim and Harker point out, the links between social class and health include other factors such as gender and ethnicity. The poverty that leads to earlier mortality and an increase in the experience of sickness and ill-health is more manifest among some ethnic groups than others. For example, not only are unemployment rates higher among black men and Pakistani and Bangladeshi men than among most white and Indian men, but wage rates are also lower among these groups. Similarly, women in these groups are both less likely to be in employment and, if they are in paid work, to receive significantly lower wages than their white counterparts (1996). These differentials have persisted as indicated by more recent evidence, for example including a widening gap in earnings among some groups such as African Caribbean men and Indian and some white groups (*Social Trends*, 2002).

People living in different socio-economic environments face very different risks of ill-health and death. In general, those at the bottom of the social scale have much poorer health than those higher up. There are inequalities in expectation of life, mortality, morbidity, and health-related behaviours amongst both adults and children, women and men, for different ethnic groups and for different migrant groups. Mortality rates, the measure of the death rate among different groups, are closely linked to social class. These rates have been measured in official statistics according to the five socio-economic categories based on paid work that have been used by the Registrar General, ranging from I and II for professional and managerial, III for skilled workers, IV for semi-skilled and V for unskilled manual workers.

This rather depressing picture was supported by various surveys of people's self-perception of their health which indicate that people in the higher social classes are far more likely than those in the lower social classes to state that they are in very good health. Morris (1995), who was a member of the 'Black Report' working group, reflecting on the findings ten years later, said that when the figures were first established they came as a shock. Although there had been differences in the life chances of the well off and the less well off ever since statistics had begun to be collected, it had been hoped that the National Health Service and the welfare state would reduce the difference. It was a shock to find that, despite 30 years of ever-increasing expenditure on the NHS, despite the many advances in medicine, there were certain groups within society whose health had not improved. In seeking the reasons for this disparity, the working group pointed to the material conditions of life – income, housing, work and general environments. These findings about people's perceptions of their own state of health, or rather ill-health, are supported by the preliminary evidence of the 2001 Census (UK Census Preliminary Report, 2003).

Like medical explanations, analyses of health and illness which focus on social factors place emphasis on structural features rather than individual health choices. However, in contrast to medical explanations, it is the structural features of *society* rather than the body which are emphasized. For example, an association between poor housing and poor health has been described since the earliest studies in the nineteenth century. While housing conditions have generally improved since this time, evidence still suggests that they are a powerful factor.

We have argued that such structural matters interrelate. Various studies were undertaken during the 1990s of Bangladeshi and Somali families who were classified as homeless and living in poor quality temporary accommodation in Tower Hamlets. They were subsequently resettled in new housing in Stepney and the Isle of Dogs. More than a year after resettlement, most families achieved a higher score on a health profile survey than they did on the same profile before the move. The reasons identified for this by the families were largely concerned with racial harassment which they said made them fearful and forced them to live restrictive lifestyles in which 'we feel like prisoners in our own homes' (Collard, 1996, p.24). This illustrates some of the ways in which different social and cultural factors combine to influence our experience of health and ill-health.

SUMMARY

According to social explanations of health and illness:

- Health and illness are not purely biological or purely social.
- The social and the biological interact to produce particular consequences for health.
- Structural factors such as class, ethnicity and gender interconnect in shaping people's experience of ill-health.
- Social analyses of health and illness drew attention to the need for restructuring the economic and physical resources of society, but did not challenge the centrality of medicine in delivering health care services.

4 COMPLEX INTERACTIONS: THE COMPLEMENTARY HEALTH MOVEMENT

So far, you may have noticed that both the medical and social analyses we have examined have talked little about health and more about illness – what causes it, how to avoid it and how to treat it. Increasingly, however, various influences combined to challenge this rather negative view which emphasized illness and began to focus more on a positive concept of health. This also marked a move away from approaches that focused on things which people share in common, such as biological endowment and social class, and an increasing emphasis on personal factors, especially the way in which we lead our individual lives. The first of these influences which we will investigate stems from what has come to be known as the complementary health movement.

There has been a considerable change in our attitude to the place of non-orthodox therapies. Only a few decades ago, therapies such as acupuncture and homeopathy were regarded as really strange, but now, if the evidence from magazines and other media is to be believed, such therapies command considerable respect. Think of the variety of herbal remedies, aromatherapy oils and so on commonly available in local chemists. A huge variety of non-orthodox therapies is now available. Some, such as Chinese acupuncture, arise from traditions whose historical origins lie further back than do those of Western medicine, whilst others, such as guided imagery, are of more recent origin. Some, such as chiropractic or osteopathy, require lengthy periods of training resulting in registration as a practitioner, whilst others, such as aromatherapy, do not.

In the 1970s, these therapies were often referred to as 'alternative' therapies, in line with that decade's discussion of 'alternative lifestyles' and notions of a rejection of mainstream values by various groups of people. However, that which might have been classified as 'alternative' has been recognized as illustrative of collective action by those resisting the constraints of the medical model. One of the best examples of this is women's action to regain control over the experience of childbirth and to categorize birth as a normal and not a medical or pathological experience. More recently, alternative therapies have gained new respectability, with many major public figures endorsing their use. It is now more common to see the term 'complementary' used by many approaches to signify that they do not reject medical diagnoses and that their techniques can be used comfortably alongside conventional medical treatment – for example, chiropractic therapy utilizes conventional anatomy and physiology. Others, however, seem to warrant the 'alternative' label. For example, homeopathy is based on the principle of treating like with like. Practitioners treat individuals with very small quantities of substances which excite similar symptoms in healthy persons to those experienced by the person who is ill, on the grounds that this stimulates the body to heal itself. This contrasts with most conventional medical treatment, which is based on the principle of allopathy, whereby illnesses are treated by drugs whose effects oppose the action of the disease.

It is difficult to estimate the size of the complementary sector since there is no single body like the National Health Service to enable the collection of statistics on numbers of practitioners, patients, frequency of consultation and so on. However, a number of studies have indicated that over the last few decades there has been an increase in the use of non-orthodox therapies and in the number and range of practitioners. In 1995, The British Medical Association estimated that one in four of the population of Britain had consulted a non-orthodox practitioner.

ACTIVITY 2.2

Have you consulted a complementary therapist? If so, why?

Even if you haven't gone to a therapist, have you used complementary aids to health such as aromatherapy? Why?

If you haven't used any form of complementary therapy, write down your reasons why not.

COMMENT

Compare any reasons you may have given for using complementary therapy with those that Ursula Sharma (1995) found in her study of the use of complementary therapies. She found that the reasons people gave for using complementary therapy fell into five groups:

- A view that conventional medicine failed to get at the 'root' cause of chronic illness or to take a preventative approach, treating the symptoms only.

- Fear of drugs becoming habit-forming or having unwelcome side-effects.

- Fear or dislike of treatments considered too radical or invasive.

- A perception that medicine failed to cope with social and experiential aspects of illness.

- Dissatisfaction with the doctor-patient relationship which gave the patient little control.

We can see from these statements that some of the elements of the medical approach to health and illness are no longer regarded as positive by some people. For instance, the medical approach of breaking the body down into parts has lead to a perception that it doesn't deal with the root causes of illness but only the symptoms. By treating the body as a biological 'machine' to be treated 'objectively', people feel doctors don't understand what it *feels* like to be ill and patients are treated as objects of diseases rather than individuals. Furthermore, rather than advances in surgery and drugs being seen as the panacea for illness, many are wary of the impact radical surgery has on their lives and of the possible side-effects of drugs.

To try to understand why complementary therapy appears to offer a positive alternative, we need to examine the underlying views about health and illness in complementary health in much the same way as we examined those for medical explanations.

4.1 The body and the mind: holistic approaches

Holistic

Holistic approaches promote ways of thinking that reject analytical or fragmented models of the world (i.e. the separation of the mind and the body) and look at component parts in combination, as a whole.

In complementary health, the body and the mind are seen as vitally related to each other and to the environment. This leads to its description as a **holistic** approach. You will recall from Section 3 that the way in which the Bangladeshi and Somali families *felt* about their new lives impacted on their health. Thus, in contrast to medical explanations, which do not see the mind as directly influencing the body, this is a key characteristic of complementary therapies. Unlike traditional medical views, where our biological nature is something to be overcome or tamed, holistic approaches view nature as a rather more benign force. Most holistic therapies place much emphasis on the healing powers of nature and natural energies. In complementary therapy, nature, in all its forms – both internal in terms of biology, feelings and emotions and external in terms of the weather, seasons and other living things – is something to be embraced. The more we are in tune with these forces, the more healthy we will be.

4.1.1 How health and illness are conceived

Holistic approaches argue that, in order to feel healthy, we need to find a balance of energies between our physical, emotional and mental aspects of health. Rather than breaking down bodies into parts, holistic approaches see things as connected and, ideally, in balance. The different forces that impact on us are neither positive nor negative in themselves, but rather finding balance is the key. No-one is either wholly ill or wholly well; even the dying may have good spiritual health. This approach applies to more than health. For example, male and female energies are seen as different, but, crucially, as balancing or complementing each other. Neither is complete without the other and both exist simultaneously in the same body. The Taoist Yin-Yang symbol is probably the best known version of this idea (see Figure 2.6). The circle of One encloses balanced opposites which contain within them small circles of their opposite.

FIGURE 2.6 The Taoist Yin-Yang symbol of balanced opposites

Each one of us has innate healing energies and the way to achieve health and a sense of well-being is to liberate these energies. Thus, in contrast to Western medicine where the emphasis is on the doctor treating illness, the task of treatment in complementary therapies is to maximize the person's access to their own healing system. There is no real gap between the knowledge of expert and layperson – what people know differs, but all knowledge is valuable and individuals can enhance and harness their knowledge of themselves. In contrast to medical ideas that focus on ideas of the body as a machine, the metaphors used by holistic therapists are rather different. Rather than seeing themselves as something akin to a mechanic, they would see themselves as more akin to a gardener. The task of therapy is to create the right climate, to give support to natural growth processes recognizing that there are seasonal changes. We can see then that holistic approaches are concerned with balancing the various forces impacting on our lives. These include the forces of nature – both our biology and the larger environment – and the forces of social organization. Thus, inherent in this approach is the notion of the interaction of natural and social forces. Neither natural nor social forces are seen as primary, but rather it is the balance between them which is crucial. Note too that holistic approaches, with their belief in the integration of the body and the mind, believe that these forces interact with the individual and we must each take responsibility for using our choices appropriately to balance the particular forces impacting upon us at any one time.

ACTIVITY 2.3

What problems with medical explanations do complementary therapies respond to?

What alternatives do they generate? Jot down a few paragraphs under these two headings:

Medical explanations – problems

Complementary explanations – alternatives

COMMENT

Medical explanations – problems	Complementary explanations – alternatives
Dualism – separation of body and mind	Holistic – integration of body and mind
Focus on illness and cure	Focus on health, well-being and prevention
Emphasis on treating the illness	Emphasis on treating the person
Doctors as experts	Therapist facilitating individual to initiate their own change
Overcoming/taming nature	Harnessing nature's positive forces

4.2 Effective understanding

You will recall from Section 2 that much of the strength of the medical view of health and illness derived from its reliance on scientific methods. Many complementary therapies are not amenable to scientific study and hence have attracted considerable criticism from doctors and other scientists and some scepticism on the part of the layperson. Advocates argue, however, that lack of scientific support for complementary therapy is not so much a criticism of the therapies themselves, but of the nature of science itself.

Science relies on systematic observation by the physical senses. In conventional medicine, illness is caused by and resides in the physical body and can be observed by doctors. In contrast, holistic complementary therapies see health and illness as a complex interaction of physical, psychological and spiritual factors which are not necessarily amenable to external study by the physical senses. Medicine's emphasis on similarities between bodies also allows it to isolate particular diseases and devise specific treatments for those diseases which can be experimentally demonstrated to be effective. In contrast, complementary therapies stress that they treat the person rather than the disease. Thus, when you consult a complementary therapist you will be asked questions, not just about your illness, but about your lifestyle, diet, stresses, things which make you happy or sad, and so on. So, if two people both have the same symptoms, whilst a conventional doctor will probably prescribe a similar treatment, a complementary therapist might suggest very different treatments for each one, taking into account the different personalities, situations and lifestyles. This emphasis on individuality makes it almost impossible to run the kind of experiment (for investigating heart-attack treatments) described in Section 2.

However, this is not to say that complementary therapy is simply based on trust or faith. An increasing number of studies describe the physiological changes which occur as a result of such therapies. For example, studies of acupuncture indicate that the various acupuncture points have different electrical potentials and affect physical structures and processes such as neurotransmitters in the brain, breathing and the immune system. So, it is clear that acupuncture needles initiate physiological change. What is not yet understandable in terms of Western science is how particular configurations of acupuncture needles produce their effects.

Whilst these criticisms focus on what are seen as difficulties complementary therapies have in demonstrating that their treatments are effective, another set of criticisms challenges the notion of nature being a benign force. Just as healing, growth and renewal are a part of nature, so too are degeneration, decay and death. Whilst we might focus on the positive and this might contribute to preventing or delaying the onset of negative natural influences, nature, like the Yin-Yang symbol in Figure 2.6, contains both positive and negative forces.

SUMMARY

In the complementary health model:

- the mind is inextricably linked to the body;

- everyone has a healing potential;

- the task of treatment is to release this potential and restore the balance in 'natural' energies;

- treatment is aimed at the whole person and hence will be different for different people;

- it is difficult to demonstrate the efficacy of treatment.

5   THE NEW PUBLIC HEALTH: THE DECLINE OF ILLNESS AND THE RISE OF HEALTH

Around the time when complementary therapies began to gain popularity and some respectability, policy makers were also reassessing the best way to maximize the health of citizens of Western industrial societies. They too began to regard health and illness as the result of diverse forces which play themselves out in complex ways. A new direction in thinking about health was heralded in 1974 when the then Canadian Minister of National Health and Welfare, Marc Lalonde, proposed that there were four distinct elements to the causes of ill health (see Bunton and Macdonald, 1992, p.9):

1   inadequacies in health care provision;

2   lifestyle or behavioural factors;

3   environmental pollution;

4   biophysical characteristics.

This more complex approach to health and illness was taken up by many governments and by the World Health Organization and launched what has become known as the 'New Public Health'. This approach recognizes the diversity of influences on health, and places much more emphasis on the promotion of health rather than the treatment of illness. The 'new' definition of health was summed up in the Ottawa Charter for Health Promotion (1987) as:

> The process of enabling people to increase control over, and to improve, their health. To reach a state of complete physical, mental and social well-being, an individual or group must be able to identify and to realise aspirations, to satisfy needs, and to change or cope with the environment ... Therefore, health promotion is not just the responsibility of the health sector ...
>
> (quoted in Davey et al., 1995, p.377)

This definition of health seems to encompass many of the factors affecting health that we have examined. Whilst acknowledging the importance of biology, it also includes social factors such as environmental pollution, adequate housing and diet, and psychological factors such as lifestyle choices. Furthermore, it shifts the view of health from an absence of illness to one that sees it as a sense of well-being. Note too that it indicates a more diverse responsibility for health. No longer are explanations couched in terms which emphasize either *structure* or *individual agency*, but rather, if we want to maximize both, then there must be action both at the level of the individual and at the level of society. It is the responsibility of health care professionals to provide adequate services and to advise people how best to make use of these services. It is the responsibility of governments to provide 'safe' and adequate environments, and it is the responsibility of individuals to choose healthy lifestyles based on sound information delivered by a variety of sources.

British policy makers were quick to take up this approach and in 1976 the Department of Health and Social Security published the document *Prevention and Health: Everybody's Business*. Whilst this ushered in policies which sought to improve social conditions such as housing, it also placed considerable emphasis on the individual's responsibility for maintaining health. The major focus was on fostering 'positive health' – in other words, to prevent illness and disease rather than to focus on treatment. The mass media were encouraged to 'market' health-enhancing behaviours such as eating healthily and taking regular exercise, whilst the government encouraged communities to develop health-enhancing environments such as providing local facilities like swimming pools and making access to exercise facilities more available.

Health promotion is directed not only at those who are sick, but also those who would regard themselves as well. For this reason, it cannot be confined to hospitals and surgeries, but has to move out into the community – to schools, workplaces, shopping centres – anywhere where people gather. In the past, attempts to improve health via community action were focused on *providing* services such as ensuring safe water supplies or adequate access to medical services. Nowadays, in a world in which we have access to many things that may have a negative impact on our health (for example, tobacco), the focus is more on persuading communities to provide circumstances which facilitate people making 'healthy' choices. Thus, to continue with the example of tobacco, as well as encouraging individuals not to smoke, many institutions have instituted 'no smoking' policies and provided employees with counselling and guidance on giving up.

Even from this brief account, some of the main lines of the New Public Health and its borrowings from other conceptions of health and illness can be discerned.

ACTIVITY 2.4

What appear to be some of the core principles of the New Public Health?

COMMENT

The core features of the New Public Health include:

- a positive and multidimensional conception of health and well-being;
- the view that health is something that is shaped by a combination of factors (social and biological; mental and physical; individual and collective);
- the view that health should be actively promoted by government, rather than focusing on curative medicine.

Two key components of the New Public Health are lifestyle and risk. This model of health acknowledges the importance of how people live their lives and the calculation of the risk which could be involved in particular lifestyles. We now look at these two aspects in more detail.

5.1 Lifestyle

The New Public Health recognized 'lifestyle or behavioural' factors as a key element in promoting health and well-being. **Lifestyle**, like health, is a complex concept with different meanings in different contexts. In sociological terms it refers to the integrated set of routine practices and decisions we engage in every day in order to function in modern society; for instance, the way we dress, what and where we eat, how and where we socialize. But lifestyle has come to mean more than simply what we do. Anthony Giddens suggests that it has taken on a meaning in terms of who we *are*. He describes lifestyle as:

> ... a more or less integrated set of practices which an individual embraces, not only because such practices fulfil utilitarian needs, but because they give material form to a particular narrative of self-identity.

> Lifestyles are routinised practices, the routines incorporated into habits of dress, eating, modes of acting and favoured milieux for encountering others; but the routines are open to change in the light of the mobile nature of self-identity. Each of the small decisions a person makes every day – what to wear, what to eat, whom to meet with later in the evening – contributes to such routines. All such choices (as well as larger and more consequential ones) are decisions not only about how to act but who to be.

> (Giddens, 1991, p.81)

Lifestyle
An integrated set of habits and practices, which both meet consumption needs and provide the basis for constructing social identities.

ACTIVITY 2.5

Let us stop for a moment and try to unpack the quotation.

Break it down into a series of distinct but interrelated claims and arguments.

C O M M E N T

1 Lifestyles can be thought of as a structured and routine pattern of social life – primarily acts of consumption, but also of interpersonal interaction.

2 Most of these acts – like eating or wearing clothes – have an obvious practical purpose. But to a considerable degree we have, in the West at any rate, choices about exactly how we do them.

3 The choices we make are also structured by questions of self-identity and personal narrative; our choices are shaped by the project of constructing a sense of who we are and who we are not in this world.

4   The repertoire of choices and patterns offered to us, the grounds on which we decide what are plausible or reasonable choices and combinations, is left open in this definition.

We can now think about changes in lifestyle using our own lives as sources of information. By adopting a particular style of dress, by buying particular kinds of food, reading particular magazines and so on, we are saying that we are a particular kind of person. In a sense, by adopting particular practices we *create* our identities (see **Woodward, 2004**).

Clearly, the creation of particular identities is associated with the consumption of particular goods and services. As you will see in Chapter 3, consumption emphasizes the individual's personal choice, and this is encouraged through 'lifestyle advertising' and 'style' TV programmes and magazines that help to define particular lifestyles and reassure us that the choices we make are reasonable and right. In relation to health, this approach emphasizes the achievement and maintenance of health as the responsibility of the individual. We are encouraged to monitor our own health and to develop healthy attitudes and behaviour.

We have seen that exhortations about healthy living don't just originate in the activities of state-sponsored health professionals, but also in a myriad of other sources from schoolteachers to supermarkets, the media and so on. There has also been an explosion of health 'resources' – be it goods such as health foods or exercise bicycles, or services such as fitness clubs and yoga classes in our local community. These affect every aspect of our lives. To take just one example, let's consider the foods we eat in the early twenty-first century.

ACTIVITY 2.6

Compare your diet now to the diet you had as a child. Think about whether there are differences in terms of the variety of foods you eat, and the way in which you prepare, cook and serve food.

Why have these changes come about? Did you change your diet consciously, prompted by information or advice of some kind?

COMMENT

Your answer to this question will vary according to your age, where you live and so on. However, our guess is that you will be eating a greater variety of foods than you did as a child, drawing on the foods of other countries and cultures. You may present your food differently now, taking more care to make it look attractive on the plate. Over the last few decades, changes in the way food is produced, stored and transported have resulted in a greater quantity and variety of foodstuffs being available all year round. We can now enjoy fresh strawberries at Christmas and we can choose between a number of different kinds, shapes and textures of tomatoes. In these circumstances, what we eat is a style choice influenced by vast numbers of cookery-books, nutritional guides and so on.

As you stand in the supermarket queue, think about what you can tell about a person's lifestyle by the kinds of food they have stacked in their trolley. We also seem to have more information about the food we eat. For instance, go to your food cupboard or freezer and take out any item of pre-packaged food. Read the label and see how, even on the most common of foods, various facts about the contents are listed.

A tin of baked beans contains more than beans! For example, a typical label lists beans, water, sugar, salt, modified cornflour, spirit vinegar, spice extracts and herb extract, and proudly claims on the label that it contains 'no artificial colours, preservatives or flavouring'.

Many writers suggest that a consequence of this emphasis on lifestyle is the notion that people are in control of their lives. They want to improve themselves and to attain or maintain good health. This view of contemporary society has important moral and political implications. It seems to suggest that we 'choose' our health through our lifestyle choices, rather than simply 'enjoying' it or 'having' it. So, rather than being something which is grounded in the structural nature of our biology or our society and thus in many respects, outside our control, health becomes a matter of individual choice and reflects our initiative, adaptability, balance and strength of will.

Several studies have demonstrated that attaining health seems to involve considerable effort. For example, when Crawford (1993) asked Americans 'Are you healthy? How do you know?', he found that good health is associated with self-discipline. When the interviewees talked about health, they included ideas like self-control, denial, discipline and willpower. They saw our current way of living as health-denying. We consume unhealthy products, lead a sedentary life, become addicted to harmful substances, and so on. Life in modern society is seen as inherently unhealthy and so to achieve health we have to exercise self-control. For these people, health is a state to be achieved and this goal competes with other goals in their lives and so it requires an active choice. If this is the view of health of ordinary people, then the next question seems to be, on what basis do we make our choices?

SUMMARY

- Behavioural and lifestyle factors contribute to the health of the individual and society.

- There is a mass of information available for people who wish to maximize their health.

- Contemporary life also allows us access to harmful substances and an unhealthy lifestyle.

- To attain health and a sense of well-being requires effort and self-control and the ability to make health changes.

5.2 Risk

Risk
The statistical likelihood of a hypothetical threat or danger occurring. Risk has come to be associated with danger more than with chance.

Like health and lifestyle, **risk** also has a range of meanings. The term 'risk' derives from statistics and refers to the probability or mathematical likelihood of a certain event occurring (e.g. that one has a one in 14 million chance of winning a lottery). In this mathematical sense the concept of risk is neutral. It simply describes a situation. However, over time the term has taken on more ominous overtones so that risk is now seen as negative. There is a tendency to believe that – while unfortunate events do happen to us – if we know the causes *and* the chances of them happening to us, then we can attempt to avoid them. In other words, risk is viewed as a means to cope with uncertainty. In recent years, there has been a proliferation of so-called 'risk factors' associated with health – the idea of there being certain things we do or are exposed to that increase the hazard or threat of illness.

ACTIVITY 2.7

Make a list of all the risk factors to health that you can think of.

Consider which ones are within your control and which ones are not within your control.

COMMENT

If your list is anything like ours, then it will include certain behaviours such as eating red meat, drinking too much, smoking, not taking enough exercise. It might also include possible risks associated with preservatives or additives in food, or another set of factors such as toxins in water, increasing levels of ultraviolet light coming through the ozone layer, pollution from cars. In some ways, it would seem that almost everything we do carries with it some form of risk. Deciding just what the risk factors are, how we should assess them and how we should overcome them has become an important enterprise at the turn of the century. The reason for this emphasis on understanding risk factors seems to be to help us as individuals to predict disease and so try to gain some control over our lives. It also seems to help society to save money since, if risk factors are reduced, people are less likely to require acute and therefore expensive medical services.

We have already noted that lifestyle is now regarded as crucial to attaining and maintaining health and that this appears to suggest that individuals are in control of their lives. Thus, if individuals choose to ignore health risks, then they are placing themselves in danger of becoming ill. Illness results in them becoming less useful members of society and also incurs expense on the health service. As we saw above, attaining health is seen by many people to require effort and gradually this 'quest for health' has come to acquire moral overtones. Those who are overweight, smokers, lazy and so on are regarded as bringing diseases such as heart attacks upon themselves. 'Self-surveillance of bodily health', as Featherstone (1991) terms it, has become a part of contemporary lifestyles. But it has also become a way for certain classes of people to distinguish themselves from other classes. Ehrenreich (1990) says that the middle classes seek out activities and artefacts which mark their distinctiveness, such as membership of executive health clubs, or eating organic food. But executive health clubs are expensive. And whilst we have noted that food of all kinds is now more abundant in our supermarkets, the very forces which have contributed to this enhanced availability, abundance and range of food have also put pressures on food producers to produce fresh food which will endure long-distance transportation and arrive fresh and tasty. Thus, many foods have additives and preservatives which many fear are injurious to their health. Increasingly, too, there is general alarm about the possible effects on health of genetically-modified foods. For these reasons, many have turned to 'natural', 'organically' produced foodstuffs. Ironically, however, these 'natural' foods tend to cost more than those that have been modified in some way. Those on fixed or low incomes may therefore be 'condemned' to eat less healthy and possibly harmful food.

The risks related to lifestyle, whilst frequently posed in terms of individuals' self-discipline and choice, can therefore be seen to be influenced by their structural position within society. Low income greatly restricts the lifestyle choices available and consequently the reduction in individual risk we are each able to make.

There also seem to be some risks which we, as individuals, find difficult if not impossible to control. The first of these are environmental risks. You will be looking further at these kinds of risks in Chapter 4 of this book, but for now let us note that the environment in which we live must allow us access to clean fresh water, clean air, shelter and a reasonable diet. Some theorists argue that affluence and overconsumption are leading us to destroy these aspects of our environment. To take just one example, the air in our cities has pollution levels that are higher than those recommended by the World Health Organization. Whilst traditional pollutants from industry and households have declined in Britain, we are now witnessing a new generation of problems. Carbon dioxide, methane and nitrous oxide are 'greenhouse gases' that are possibly contributing to climate instability. The long-term effects on health of such instabilities are difficult to assess but are likely to be profound. Meanwhile, another example is the depletion of the ozone layer which is likely to increase the incidence of skin cancer.

Whilst the New Public Heath does not place sole reliance on medicine to maximize the health of the nation, nevertheless our biological characteristics and the role of doctors are still regarded as crucial. As health education has become more widespread, the media have played a vital role in 'educating' public opinion. Medical sections in newspapers, magazines and television programmes have become commonplace. Information is provided to make expert medical knowledge available to large numbers of people. Whilst for the most part this can be seen as a positive move, it does have some drawbacks. A subject which has attracted much media attention, but which exemplifies the dangers of oversimplification of the implications of risk reduction in the media, is genetic screening.

Although genetic screening has been available for many years, media interest was intensified when the Human Genome Project was initiated. This is a project designed to map the 1,000,000 or so genes that comprise human DNA, which is contained in every cell of our body. It is intended to identify every gene sequence in our body, and it is hoped that such identification might help us to understand genetic causes of a variety of diseases from mental illness to cancer.

But there are problems with much of this media coverage. It is not a simple matter of discovering *the* gene for cancer. Usually, diseases are caused by particular *sequences* of genes, and there are almost endless permutations of these sequences. In addition, as we saw in Chapter 1 of this book, social and environmental factors affect whether or not a particular genetic trait is expressed in the body. In other words, even though an individual might possess a particular gene or combination of genes, it doesn't necessarily show itself in the body without a particular social or physical environment. So genetic screening is not as simple as the media would often seem to suggest. It is not just a matter of identifying 'natural' forces, but rather one of understanding how these natural forces interact with forces in our physical and social environments.

Furthermore, as in the case of lifestyles, genetic screening carries with it serious ethical and moral issues for both individuals and for society as a whole. If screening reveals that someone possesses an 'undesirable' gene and that there is a likelihood of this gene being passed on to their children, then the individual has to make difficult decisions about whether or not to reproduce. Genetic screening also has the potential to detect the likelihood of contracting or developing disease later in life. This may be positive for the individual concerned, in that they may be able to change their lifestyle, diet and so on and delay onset. However, if this information is made more widely available, then the potential for serious problems ensues. If, for example, all new employees had to submit to genetic screening, they might be refused employment based only on the probability of them developing a disease at some stage. The late twentieth century witnessed the difficulties of those who have been tested as HIV positive and who often experience difficulty in obtaining employment, insurance and access to many aspects of life we all take for granted.

This oversimplified media coverage of genetic screening also has the potential to undermine the more diverse explanation of health that has gained ground in the late twentieth century. Genes are frequently described as 'coding' for particular functions or attributes, thereby reinstating the dominance of biological explanations without giving due account to individual choice, social and environmental factors. As we hope you will now appreciate, explanations that do not recognize and give due account to the diverse influences on health are unlikely to be satisfactory.

The above analysis makes clear that understanding risk and dealing with it is a very difficult business. It involves a complex mix of internal and external factors over which individuals have varying levels of control. The New Public Health model suggests that risk reduction is best enhanced by efforts to:

- encourage individuals to reduce their own health risks;
- support actions of organizations, communities, local, national and international governments to reduce external risks and provide conditions under which individuals can be encouraged to reduce their own risk.

But it must also be recognized that there are considerable difficulties, including:

- providing information in a way which enables individuals to make sense of the proposed risks;
- reorganizing society so that individuals can have equal access to risk reduction;
- presenting information on risk reduction in such a way that the existence of a probability does not exclude people from everyday activities;
- recognizing that action on environmental risk reduction must be orchestrated between societies as well as within individual societies.

SUMMARY

- The New Public Health model was a response to the limits of the social model.
- It introduced a much more multidimensional, multi-factor model of health.
- It draws on the notions of lifestyle and risk to make good some of the weaknesses in the social model.
- It alerts us to the importance of the external natural environment and pollution risks on health.
- It relies on risk assessment calculators whose claims are open to criticism.
- It advocates a less redistributive and more individualized, culturally focused set of health policies.

6 CONCLUSION

So what have we found out in our tour of conceptions of health and illness since the end of the Second World War? In particular, as the title of the chapter asks, *whose health is it anyway?* As one of the authors of this chapter, I began its exploration of health and illness by considering my asthma, asking what causes it and how best I can control it and reduce its effects on my everyday life. Let's explore this through the various explanations we have encountered.

ACTIVITY 2.8

Write notes in the grid on the emphasis each of the explanations we have examined would place on:

- natural or social explanations of asthma;

- whether managing it is within the individual's control.

	Medical	Social	Complementary	New Public Health
Natural/ social	Natural	Social	Natural	Social
Individual control	Social	Natural	Social	Social

COMMENT

In the middle years of the twentieth century, medicine would have viewed asthma as primarily a natural condition – a result of my biological heritage. Thus, it was not within my control and so the best way of dealing with its effects was to hand myself over to doctors. Because doctors have at their disposal instruments and techniques to look inside the body and see how the physiological process of asthma works in lots of bodies, then they could run experiments to test for the best treatment. According to this medical view, all I really need to do is to comply with their instructions.

By the 1980s, social analyses prompted additional questions about the effect of social environments on the incidence of illness. These analyses, like those of medicine, looked for regularities, for patterns of health and illness in relation to particular social groups. Thus, asthma might be demonstrated to be related to, for example, damp housing conditions. If such an association was found, then pressure might be brought to bear on governments and housing associations to improve the standard of housing. Maximizing health in this approach was not aimed at the individual, but rather at improving conditions for everyone, with the assumption that this would improve health overall, and what residual illnesses were left over could best be dealt with by doctors. So if moving to a better home didn't cure my asthma, recourse to medicine and drugs was still seen to be the way forward.

Around this time, however, a variety of alternatives to drugs for dealing with asthma began to attract publicity. A huge number of different therapies were on offer – from acupuncture to aromatherapy, to herbs, to relaxation. Whilst doctors tend to define someone like me as an asthmatic, these complementary therapists would view me as a person with asthma. Instead of focusing only on the asthma, they would take into account a variety of other things about my life. In their view, asthma is not an inevitable result of either biological heritage or social environment. Rather, it is a result of an imbalance in the various physical, social, psychological, spiritual and environmental forces surrounding the individual. Some complementary therapists, such as acupuncturists, intervene physically to help balance those energies. Others, such as relaxation therapists, encourage meditation and making choices which encourage a sense of well-being. Such complementary approaches seems to accord the individual some control over his or her asthma, but the emphasis on the whole individual means that the evidence that complementary therapies produce for their efficacy cannot have the same degree of certainty as is provided by scientific explanations.

The New Public Health also seems to accord high value to balance and, like complementary medicine, suggests that conditions such as asthma are caused by complex interactions between biological, social and environmental, and individual factors. However, because it is primarily aimed at the level of policy, it looks for evidence which is based on regularities and patterns and so utilizes some of the techniques of the scientific approach. But it also accords some degree of control to the individual and seeks to provide social and environmental conditions which are conducive to health and which allow the individual to make sensible, healthy choices. In this view, asthma is neither a natural nor a social phenomenon, nor a result of entirely structural or individual factors. Rather, the boundaries between these polarized explanations have become increasingly blurred. Instead of focusing on which has the most power, research under the New Public Health is increasingly aimed towards understanding the way in which these interactions play themselves out in societies as a whole and within the individual. Considerable research has focused on identifying various risk factors to health which need attention, both by national and international governments and by individuals and groups. In this view then, my asthma is a complex interaction of natural and social forces and is affected by both structural and individual factors. Whilst the fact that I have asthma is not my 'fault', there are things I can do to reduce its effects.

ACTIVITY 2.9

To help you consolidate your understanding of each of the approaches to health which have been presented in this chapter, and to help you engage in the important task of comparing and contrasting them, have a go at answering the following questions by completing the table overleaf. Our notes are included at the end of the chapter to help you if you get stuck.

	Medical approach	Social approach	Complementary approach	New Public Health approach
Emphasis on natural or social				
Definition of health and illness				
Causes of illness				
Implications for health services				
Sources of evidence				
Role of social structures and individual agency				

- What is the balance of natural and social forces in shaping people's health?
- How does each approach define health and illness?
- What does each see as the causes of health and illness?
- What are the implications for health services?
- What is the source of evidence for each approach?
- To what extent do individual choices and agency as opposed to social structures shape people's health?

So it seems that there are lots of different ways of answering the questions as to who or what is responsible for our health. These different ways are based on different concepts of what health and illness are, and from these conceptions flow different ways of dealing with illness and promoting health. No single explanation seems to have all the answers. Each has its strengths and weaknesses. What is clear though is that health is a major concern both to individuals and to societies as a whole and research and investigation will continue in variety of spheres. What we hope you will be able to do as new ideas and evidence emerge is to view them critically, examining their basic assumptions, the kinds of evidence they produce, the kinds of explanation they offer and the kinds of intervention they suggest. We hope too that you will be alert to considering the possible ethical and moral issues they raise.

REFERENCES

British Medical Association (1986) *Report of the Board of Science and Education on Alternative Medicine*, London, BMA.

Bunton, R. and Macdonald, G. (1992) 'Health promotion: discipline or disciplines?' in Bunton, R. and Macdonald, G. (eds) *Health Promotion: Disciplines and Diversity*, London, Routledge.

Collard, A. (1996) *Homing In: Providing for the Health and Resettlement Needs of Rehoused Homeless Families*, Oxford, THHSG.

Crawford, R. (1993) 'A cultural account of "health": control, release and the social body' in Beattie, A., Gott, M., Jones, L. and Sidell, M. (eds) *Health and Wellbeing: A Reader*, Houndmills, Macmillan.

Davey, B., Gray, A. and Seale, C. (eds) (1995) *Health and Disease*, Buckingham, Open University Press.

Department of Health and Social Security (1976) *Prevention and Health: Everybody's Business*, London, HMSO.

Ehrenreich, B. (1990) *The Fear of Falling: The Inner Life of the Middle Class*, New York, Harper Perennial.

Featherstone, M. (1991) 'The body in consumer culture' in Featherstone, M., Hepworth, M. and Turner, B.S. (eds) *The Body: Social Process and Cultural Theory*, London, Sage.

Giddens, A. (1991) *Modernity and Self-Identity: Self and Society in the Late Modern Age*, Cambridge, Polity.

Morris, J.N. (1995) 'Inequalities in health: ten years and little further on' in Davey, B., Gray, A. and Seale, C. (eds).

Oppenheim, C. and Harker, L. (1996) *Poverty: The Facts*, London, Child Poverty Action Group.

Ottawa Charter for Health Promotion (1987) *Health Promotion*, vol.1, no.4, p.iii.

Sharma, U. (1995) 'Using alternative therapies: marginal medicine and central concerns' in Davey, B., Gray, A. and Seale, C. (eds).

Social Trends, London, HMSO (annual).

UK Census Preliminary Report (2003) at www.statistics.gov.uk (accessed February 2003).

Whitehead, M. (1992) 'The health divide' in *Inequalities in Health*, Harmonsworth, Penguin.

Woodward, K. (2004) 'Questions of identity' in Woodward, K. (ed.) *Questioning Identity: Gender, Class, Ethnicity* (2nd edn), London, Routledge/The Open University.

FURTHER READING

There is an enormous body work on health and illness in the social sciences.

Margaret Whitehead's edited collection *Inequalities in Health* (1992, Harmondsworth, Penguin) is the central point of reference for all debates around social explanations.

For an accessible and critical overview of complementary explanations, see Ros Coward's *The Whole Truth* (1990, London, Faber and Faber).

On the New Public Health and discussions of risk, an excellent overview is provided by Deborah Lupton's *The Imperative of Health: Public Health and the Regulated Body* (1995, London, Sage).

Michael Hardy's *The Social Context of Health* (1998, Buckingham, Open University Press) provides a useful introduction to the concerns of health psychology and includes an overview of the history of medical explanations.

COMMENT ON ACTIVITY 2.9 _____

	Medical approach	Social approach	Complementary approach	New Public Health approach
Emphasis on natural or social	Natural	Social	More natural: mind and body viewed holistically	Both. Interrelationship between natural and social
Definition of health and illness	Emphasis on illness: health defined as absence of disease	Emphasis on illness	Emphasis on health	Emphasis on health, but recognition of importance of treating illness
Causes of illness	Biological factors	Social factors	Imbalance	Natural and social, exposure to risk
Implications for health services	Doctors, hospitals, 'experts'	Redistribute economic resources	Therapists as facilitators	Health responsibility of all: governments and business responsible for providing healthy environment, individuals responsible for making healthy choices
Sources of evidence	Scientific experiments	Statistical surveys	Personal efficacy	Risk assessments
Role of social structures and individual agency	Emphasis on biological structures and agency of individual doctors	Emphasis on social structures	Emphasis on personal agency	Combination of social and biological structures and individual agency, e.g. lifestyle and risk assessments

Nature for sale

Susan Himmelweit and Roberto Simonetti

chapter 3

Contents

1   THE 'NATURAL' ENVIRONMENT

As we discovered in the previous two chapters of this book, drawing the distinction between what is social and what is natural is harder than it first looks. We found social and natural factors to be inextricably connected in explaining both our lives as human beings and our health. In this chapter we shall move outwards from ourselves to examine the natural environment 'outer nature', an aspect of 'nature' that apparently lies outside and might be independent of us, existing prior to human intervention. In doing so, we shall reflect the increasing concern in recent years about the destructive effects of human beings on the natural environment, and consider the interrelation of the social and the natural in creating such problems.

ACTIVITY 3.1

What do you mean by the natural environment? Take a few minutes to write down ten words that the term 'natural environment' suggests to you.

Our list includes a mix of different types of things. There are examples of non-human resources, such as forests and fish stocks, that, in the past, people tended to assume they could use as they liked; now there is concern that stocks are not being sufficiently replenished (see Figure 3.1). The environment, then, is something we can use up.

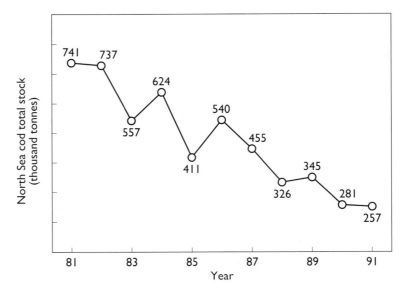

FIGURE 3.1   Fish stocks in the North Sea 1981–1991

Water and air are on our list too. They are there because they are important constituent parts of the context in which we all live our lives. We do not each have our own patch of clean air; we share the air we breathe and our water comes from a common source. The problem here is that the activities of a few people can contaminate such **shared resources** for everyone. We all breathe the same air and, unless we go to the expense of buying bottled water, depend upon the same water supplies. The environment, then, is something that we all share and can spoil for each other.

On our list we also have the climate and the beauty of unspoiled countryside. These are like clean air in that we all share the climate, but the climate seems to be subject to more long-term influences and changes more slowly. So, depending on which forecast of the effects of global warming you look at, our worries about the climate may be less about what will happen in our own life times, and more about the conditions under which future generations will live. The environment, then, is something that we can damage for the future.

The items on your list probably differ from ours, but we would be surprised if your list did not contain some similar examples of stocks that are being depleted, shared resources that are being spoiled and aspects of the world around us that we could damage for future generations. And, like our list, we expect that yours reflects current concerns. Our list does not include the stock of flies, for example, because we have not read of any serious concerns about diminishing stocks of flies and we are not particularly fond of flies ourselves. Similarly, although we all depend on the sun more fundamentally perhaps than anything else, our list does not include it as part of the environment. Though the sun is obviously an important shared resource that we do not want spoiled and without which future generations could not exist, we do not know of anything that people are currently doing that has been thought to threaten the sun in any way that would have serious consequences for us now or in the future. When talking about the natural environment, we tend to include only those areas of the natural world on which people are having or might have an effect, and where consequent changes may, in turn, adversely affect us. There are other approaches to the natural environment that are more ecological and less human-centred, but, in practice, our more human-centred or 'social' approach is used in most political debates about the environment. This is another example of where the natural and the social are inextricably intertwined, in this case, in what we even recognize as the 'natural' environment.

We have probably never been so aware of how our actions can damage the environment as we are now at the beginning of the twenty-first century. Interest in the environment has steadily increased over the last twenty or thirty years, and a number of 'green' organizations (from non-government pressure groups, such as Greenpeace, to influential political parties such as the German Greens) have ensured that governments that are keen to retain votes must address environmental issues.

Shared resources
Resources that are not privately owned by anybody and whose use is freely shared.

A number of factors lie behind the emergence of this green consciousness, including some large-scale environmental disasters provoked by human actions such as the deadly gas leak from the Union Carbide plant in Bhopal that killed thousands and left many more permanently disabled, and increasing worries about nuclear power since the Chernobyl disaster. Had you heard of Chernobyl before it sent a radioactive cloud over Europe and beyond?

Such environmental accidents have made people realize that human technology can have devastating and irreversible effects on the environment. However, many green organizations worry more about the less spectacular but more widespread environmental degradation that seems to accompany normal economic growth. The unprecedented economic growth that industrialized market economies, such as Britain, have experienced over the last two hundred years seems to have led not only to much higher levels of consumption, but also to the degradation of the natural environment.

ACTIVITY 3.2

Figure 3.2 is a line chart that illustrates the economic growth of the UK, the US and Japan from 1820 to 1989. The indicator used, GDP per person, roughly measures the amount of goods and services produced per person in a country.

What information does this figure provide?

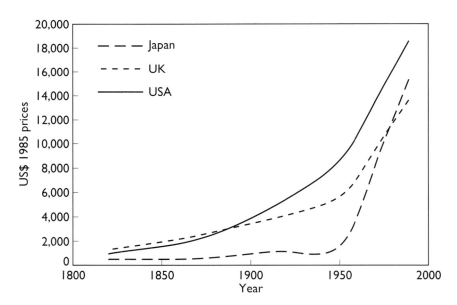

FIGURE 3.2 Economic growth in UK, US and Japan; GDP per person
Source: Maddison, 1991, Table A.2, pp.198, Tables B.l, B.2, B.3 and B.4, pp.226–39

Each line in the chart tracks the value of **GDP** per person over time for the three countries – UK, US and Japan – from 1820 to 1989. (The 'legend' allows you to identify which country each line represents.) The lines rise for all countries over the years in the period considered, showing that **economic growth** has been a key feature of the last two centuries for these industrialized countries. You can see that the slopes of the lines become even steeper from 1950. This indicates that, on average, the increase in GDP per person was greater in the years since 1950 than in the years before it.

A similar picture emerges from Table 3.1 which reports the average yearly rates of growth for the same three countries over the same period.

GDP (Gross Domestic Product)
Measures the total quantity of goods and services produced in a country in a period of time (usually a year).

A country's economic growth
The expansion of a country's economy, which is often measured by the rate of change of GDP or GDP per person.

TABLE 3.1   Economic growth in Japan, UK and US: average yearly rate of growth of GDP per person in selected periods (per cent)

Country	1820–70	1870–1913	1913–50	1950–73	1973–89
Japan	0.1	1.4	0.9	8.0	3.1
UK	1.2	1.0	1.0	2.5	1.8
US	1.5	1.9	1.6	2.2	1.6

Source: Maddison, 1991, Table A.2, pp.198, Tables B.I, B.2, B.3 and B.4, pp.226–39

You can see from the table that, on average, growth was highest in the period between 1950 and 1973, when the yearly rate of growth has the highest value for all three countries (and especially for Japan, which shows an astonishing rate of growth of 8 per cent). It is not surprising, therefore, that many concerns about the effect of economic growth on the environment started emerging in the 1960s.

Most environmental degradation is not the result of anybody consciously deciding to pollute the atmosphere or run down fish stocks. Rather, when we talk about environmental degradation, we mean the unintended consequences of actions whose intended effects are quite different and may be wholly beneficial. When people have a primary purpose of creating harm we do not talk about it as environmental degradation, rather we see it as an act of vandalism or war. And, usually, governments have not set out to promote environmental damage. Most now claim to be committed to environmental protection and improvement. However, despite such commitments, the general consensus is that environmental degradation is getting worse not better.

Some unintended consequences are simply the result of ignorance. People did not know that certain gases, such as CFCs, might cause the problems that we now believe they do. But if ignorance was the only problem, then people would stop as soon as they understood the harmful consequences of their actions. The problem lies deeper, in that people, firms and states may even knowingly continue to cause environmental degradation, precisely because their primary purpose is elsewhere. Environmental degradation, then, is a regrettable by-product of their primary activities, but the imperative that drives those primary activities has much more force than concern for the environmental consequences. And this applies at all levels of society: whenever people drive to work because it is more convenient than taking public transport; whenever firms pollute rivers with their waste because it is cheaper than a cleaner production method; or whenever governments allow oil companies to despoil parts of the countryside because they fear the electoral consequences of raising direct taxes rather than relying on oil revenues. In all these cases, environmental degradation is a by-product of other actions carried out by people and organizations who, in their particular circumstances, do not consider avoiding the consequent environmental degradation to be worth abandoning their primary objective. For them, at least, the gains outweigh the losses.

In this way, environmental degradation has been the by-product of economic growth in the past and continues to be so in many ways, despite a greater awareness of environmental issues. Some see environmental degradation as the inevitable counterpart of economic growth; so that the only way to protect the environment would be to slow down or even cease economic growth. Others argue that environmental degradation is not an inevitable by-product of economic growth, but has happened because of the way economic activity is organized in modern industrial economies, and we could have sustainable economic growth that is environmentally friendly if we organized it differently. For them, the culprit is not growth itself, but the way growth is currently organized through markets.

Market forces
This refers to a characteristic of competitive markets, in which economic agents are not free to set prices and must buy or sell at prices given by the market.

Market economy
An economy in which resources are mainly allocated through exchange in markets.

In markets, people tend to look after their own interests and in doing so they neglect the environmental consequences of their actions. For example, environmentally safe methods of pest control, or at least ones that are much safer than those used today, have been available since the early 1960s. They are not applied because other environmentally less desirable methods of pest control are less costly and generate higher profits for the people who decide what pesticides to use. It is not that the people making these choices are inherently greedy. Rather, they have little choice. **Market forces** ensure that firms that do not choose the most efficient, that is the least costly and thus the most profitable, methods of production will not survive. This is because in competitive markets, firms with high costs can only sell without a loss if they set a high price, but buyers will not buy their products if more efficient competitors charge a lower price for the same item. So in a **market economy** it is no use appealing to people's better nature. Economic organizations, such as firms, have no choice but to choose the least costly methods of production – and so if some of the costs can be off-loaded onto the environment they will be. The market is a structure and the people and organizations that operate within it have to live by its rules – the rules of market forces – or die.

According to this argument, environmental degradation is not an inevitable consequence of growth in *all* circumstances, but of growth in an unregulated market economy. This suggests that there might be ways in which the economy can be changed and the action of market forces modified so that they work to protect rather than destroy the environment. Whether market forces can be modified to environmentally beneficial ends is a subject of intense political debate.

This chapter aims to give you some of the economic background to that debate. First we need to look at how the market works when it works well, so in Section 2 we examine how the argument could be made that a market allocates resources in the best possible way. Section 3 looks at how models can be used to investigate the ideas behind the theories and Section 4 goes on to investigate the model of the market using a worked example. In Section 5, in contrast, we look at why this model does not hold for all types of resources, including many natural resources, and what would need to be done to modify the operation of markets in these cases. This should leave you in a position, in Section 6, to assess the economic and political arguments for and against the idea that it is possible to modify or regulate a market economy so that it protects, rather than harms, the natural environment.

SUMMARY

- Environmental problems are generated at the interface of nature and society.

- Environmental problems include using up stocks of exhaustible resources, misusing shared resources and ignoring the interests of future generations.

- Historically there has been a link between economic growth and environmental degradation, at least in market economies.

- In such economies, the market is a structure within which people must operate. Sometimes they have little choice but to act in environmentally unfriendly ways if they are to survive in a market economy.

- This raises the question of whether markets can be modified in ways that would enable people to protect rather than harm the environment.

2 MARKETS AND THE 'INVISIBLE HAND'

In the previous section we raised the question of whether environmental problems were the inevitable by-product of economic growth in a market economy. By a market economy we mean an economy in which the main way in which resources are allocated is through markets. To answer that question we have to understand what is meant by a market and how markets allocate resources.

How would you define a market? What is the main activity that goes on in a market? What distinguishes one market from another?

You may have thought of local fruit and vegetable markets, big shopping centres or even car boot sales. In these cases, the idea of a market conjures up a physical place where many buyers and sellers come together to trade goods and services, exchanging them usually for money. *Exchange* is certainly central to the definition of any market. But to define the market as a place where goods and services are traded is too restrictive because there are many different ways in which exchange can happen, not all of which require buyers and sellers to meet in one place, for example we can buy a book by going to a local shop, by post through a catalogue or at home on the Internet.

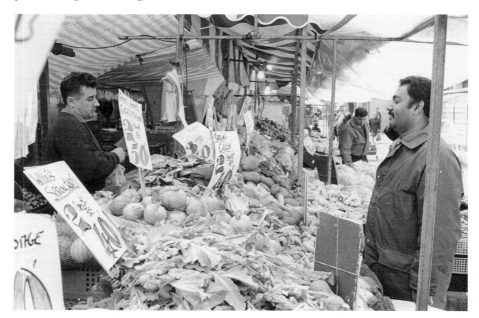

FIGURE 3.3   Not all markets are like this local fruit and vegetable market where buyers and sellers meet in one place

Markets also differ according to what is exchanged; buying a second-hand car is very different from buying a pension or the services of a childminder. So we define a **market** by the commodity that is exchanged in it, and talk about 'the market' for second-hand cars, for pensions or for childcare. According to this definition, shopping centres are not markets, but places where parts of many markets operate. Markets can have geographical boundaries – we can talk, for instance, about the differences between the American and Japanese labour markets, but some markets have no boundaries – for example global markets exist for some commodities such as crude oil or copper.

A market consists of *buyers* and *sellers* that trade in its commodity; these are known as economic agents. An **economic agent** does not have to be an individual, it can be any entity that can come to a decision and act upon it; so organizations such as firms, households, charities and governments, as well as individual people, are economic agents. In order to trade, agents have to *interact* in some way, not necessarily face to face; networked computers, for example, are widely used in financial markets. Markets also need trading rules and conventions to regulate the way agents interact; these are social institutions that may vary between one market and another. However, one institution that is common to nearly all markets in a modern economy is the use of money. Instead of being directly exchanged (bartered) for each other, commodities are usually exchanged for money and have a price expressed in money terms. Money is a social institution that only works when people accept that it is exchangeable against all other goods and that it will not lose its value.

A sale results in the transfer of **property rights** in a commodity from seller to buyer. Property rights usually give owners the right to use and dispose of their property. However, there are some types of property where ownership does not confer both these rights. For example, without planning permission we cannot use houses we own just as we like. Other property cannot be disposed of, for example the properties that the National Trust owns are inalienable, this means that they cannot be given away or sold. In general, however, people have the right both to use their own property as they like and to sell it. If you do not want to use something that you own, it makes sense to exchange it with someone else who has something you do want. This is the rationale behind the propensity 'to truck, barter and exchange' that Adam Smith, the Scottish philosopher who is considered to be the founder of modern economics, saw as the basis of a modern economy.

Markets also differ in the number and types of agents who trade in them. In some markets, such as telecommunications, only a few large companies sell goods and services, whereas in others a myriad of sellers compete without even knowing of each other's existence. In markets where there are many buyers and sellers, no single agent is likely to have much influence over what goes on. In particular they will not be able to do much about the prices at which they can buy or sell. It appears, then, that the market itself determines prices and therefore the possibilities that are open to buyers and sellers. All agents in such

A market
A market comprises all the exchanges involving a certain type of commodity (often within a defined geographical area).

Economic agent
An entity, such as an individual, a firm or a government, that can make economic decisions and act upon them.

Property rights
The rights of owners to use and dispose of their goods.

competitive markets feel themselves subject to market forces and will survive only if they are efficient. If there are few sellers in a market (or even only one) each seller will have power to influence prices, and market forces will not be quite so constraining. This is why governments usually regulate such markets, or try to promote competition in order to impose the discipline of market forces on monopolies. Similar problems arise in markets where there are few buyers.

SUMMARY

- In markets, agents exchange property rights over a commodity, usually for a price paid in money.
- Markets are defined according to the commodity exchanged (in some cases within a certain geographical boundary).
- An economic agent is any entity that can make economic decisions and act upon them. Governments, firms, individuals, charities and trade unions can all be economic agents.
- Markets in which there are many buyers and sellers are competitive. In such markets, no individual agent has much power and 'market forces' determine prices.

2.1 The neoclassical theory of what markets do best

Economists, from Adam Smith in the eighteenth century onwards, have praised the way in which markets have contributed to the achievement of greater human prosperity. In his book *The Wealth of Nations*, Smith introduces his famous 'invisible hand' as a metaphor for how markets work to co-ordinate the self-interested actions of agents to the common good.

Modern neoclassical economists, who form the dominant mainstream school in economics today, have continued Smith's work by trying to clarify the conditions under which markets work well and what benefits they deliver. In their view, one of the main benefits of markets is that, under the right conditions, markets will allocate existing resources to satisfy current human wants in the most efficient way. In this it is assumed that all important 'wants' can be satisfied by the consumption of goods and services, and generally that all 'resources' are privately owned. We will see later the extent to which neoclassical analysis can be applied to resources that are not privately owned and can be spoiled by current use or, like fossil fuels, are non-renewable. We look at whether this analysis can take account of 'wants' that cannot be satisfied by consumption.

The neoclassical view of the market focuses on how, in a market economy, choices made by vast numbers of economic agents, each following their own interests, result in goods and services being produced that make those choices feasible. It assumes that consumers, given their incomes and current prices, decide what to buy self-interestedly according to their tastes, without considering the wider effects of their actions. Similarly, firms decide what to produce and what resources to use according to what is profitable to them at current prices, given the technology to which they have access and the prices they must pay for the resources they use, again without considering any wider effects. Given this, how do markets ensure that all those decisions are co-ordinated efficiently so that agents, prepared to accept current prices, can find what they want to buy or sell? In the neoclassical view, markets alone can achieve an impressive degree of co-ordination through the working of the **price mechanism**.

Prices provide economic agents with incentives to use resources efficiently by collecting all relevant information and conveying it efficiently. If, for example, a bad harvest in Brazil leads to a shortage of coffee, there will be insufficient coffee available to satisfy all consumers who want to drink coffee at the existing price. Sellers then find they can raise the price of coffee and still sell it. Buyers experience a rise in the price of coffee and only those who are willing to pay more for it (either those who particularly like drinking coffee or have more money to spend) will now buy it. So when the price of coffee rises, consumers are given an incentive to consume less coffee and switch to drinking something else. This will result in less coffee being sold, but those customers willing to pay the new higher price will still be able to drink it – the price rises until it has persuaded just the right number to spend their money elsewhere and *all* customers willing to buy coffee at the new price will be satisfied. Similarly, if the price has risen only just the right amount, there will be no sellers left with coffee still to sell. Coffee consumption will be reduced without coffee drinkers needing to know the cause of the shortage.

So prices direct the allocation of goods towards those consumers who value them more, that is, those who are willing to pay more for them. Producers also look at prices in order to decide what and how much to produce. If the production of a good is not profitable because too few consumers want it and therefore the price is too low to make a profit, producers switch to the production of a good for which demand is high. If too many producers want to produce the same good, however, they will have to compete in order to win customers; they will do so by offering to sell at a lower price. If the price of coffee falls, for example, some producers will decide that it is no longer worth producing coffee; these will be the least efficient coffee producers, that is, those with the highest costs. In this way, the movement of prices ensures that coffee is produced by the most efficient producers, and drunk by those consumers who value it most.

All information about both the resources needed to produce a good (like coffee) and the value that consumers place on the consumption of that good is summarized in the price of the good. So, the price of a good reflects both the costs of the resources needed to produce it and the value that consumers put on its consumption. These producers and consumers might be spread out throughout the world and most will never meet each other, but the world price for coffee, for example, will reflect all these different conditions in a

Price mechanism
The way in which prices co-ordinate the actions of buyers and sellers in markets by providing them with information and incentives that shape their decisions, and the way in which all buyers' and all sellers' actions together determine prices.

single number. According to this account, the price mechanism enables markets to use all the relevant information available in the economy efficiently to allocate resources.

It is this ability of the market to co-ordinate the economy without the knowledge or intervention of people that led Adam Smith to talk about the price mechanism as if it was an 'invisible hand'. He was impressed by how an economy consisting of a myriad of producers all behaving in their own self-interest, that is, trying to make as much profit as possible without considering the effects on other people, did not collapse into anarchy. Instead there would be a functioning market in which customers could purchase whatever they wanted, provided they would pay the going price, and producers could sell all their goods at that price.

SUMMARY

- Neoclassical economists claim that the market allocates existing resources in an efficient way, by which they mean that goods are allocated to the consumers who are willing to pay most for them, and are produced by the most efficient producers, that is, those with the lowest costs.

- The price mechanism is central to the functioning of markets. Prices are determined by the interaction of consumers' and producers' decisions.

- Prices co-ordinate the actions of economic agents in markets by providing sufficient incentives and information on which agents can base their decisions. The final outcome of the decisions made by agents based on prices is an efficient allocation of resources.

- Adam Smith saw the price mechanism as the 'invisible hand' that allowed the market, without human intervention, to co-ordinate the behaviour of producers acting in their own self interest, in such a way that consumers' needs were satisfied.

3 MODELLING MARKETS

Model
A model is a simplified representation of reality in which only the essential elements of the social process under investigation are included.

The neoclassical theory of how markets work to allocate resources efficiently is an example of an economic **model**. It is not an easy task to describe how all markets work because markets differ in the type of commodity exchanged, in the trading rules that are observed and in the number and type of agents that participate in them. Nevertheless, all markets have some common characteristics and it is these that neoclassical economists have used to build their model of the market. In other words, they have selected some basic features that characterize markets and the behaviour of agents in markets to show how a simplified, ideal market works.

Model building is extensively used in social sciences to investigate social processes. Models are simplified representations of reality which focus on the features common to different instances of that process (in this case agents buying and selling in markets) and everything that is not essential to the understanding of the process under investigation is left out. When we build a model, we consider only the essential characteristics of the phenomenon studied; other characteristics that are deemed to be unimportant, that is, those that are thought not to influence the process examined, are left out. Which characteristics are important, in turn, depends on the specific purposes of the investigator.

Although we do not talk about them that way, we build models every time we try to explain any causal relationship. If I claim to have an explanation of how traffic fumes cause children's asthma, I mean that I have a general story that runs from some significant constituents of traffic fumes, through to a picture of how the human respiratory system works, to what produces the symptoms of asthma. However, you would not expect me to start my explanation by telling you how particles in the exhaust fumes of the number 37 bus ended up in a particular child's lungs and the effects that they had on her air passages before going on to list the effects of every other vehicle on every other child's breathing problems. You would expect me to talk about the connection between exhaust fumes in general and asthma in particular, that is, to build a model that simplifies in order to get away from the detail. In order to get away from the complex detail of reality, we have to try to find general features to characterize any particular process we want to understand and leave out the messy details from the picture.

In order to be useful, models have to be parsimonious – that is, composed of few elements and relationships. If a model is too complex, the basic processes get lost in the detail – it becomes a case of not being able to see the wood for the trees. However, models must still preserve all the fundamental characteristics necessary to understand the process being investigated. So, a model builder must strike a balance between simplicity and comprehensiveness.

Models can be expressed both in sophisticated mathematical notation and through everyday language. The neoclassical explanation of how the price mechanism works to allocate resources to satisfy consumers' wishes that you met in Section 2.1 was a model expressed solely in words, in which the movement of prices played a fundamental role. However, there was also a hidden simplifying assumption that there was a single price for each commodity. This in itself needs explanation; why should we expect to pay similar prices when we buy a particular good? Section 4 outlines a different type of model, one which uses a numerical example to illustrate the process by which a market arrives at a single price for a commodity. The model also shows why that price can be seen as the 'right' one for the commodity, given the particular characteristics of buyers and sellers in the market.

S U M M A R Y

- A model is a simplified representation of reality used to understand causal relationships within social processes.

- A model should leave out everything that is not seen as essential to the process under investigation.

- Models must be simple enough to be understandable and comprehensive enough to include all the features relevant to explaining the process being investigated.

4   HOW PRICES ARE FORMED

The model in this section is designed to illustrate how prices are formed. It looks at a market for a good that doesn't differ in its quality, and in which there are just five potential producers and five potential consumers. Because it is convenient to give the good a name, we'll call it a loaf of bread. We know that, in practice, loaves of bread differ in all sorts of ways, but those in our model do not. Ignoring the different qualities of the bread is a simplification that is designed to aid our understanding, but sufficient complexity is left in our model in order for us to learn about the price mechanism.

For the price mechanism to work, producers and consumers must differ among themselves. Some producers can produce a loaf of bread more efficiently and thus more cheaply than others. Perhaps the more efficient producers use newer machinery or have a more skilled workforce, or perhaps they are only more 'efficient' because they use a cheaper sort of wheat that is produced using some environmentally undesirable pesticides. For whatever the reason, their **unit costs** vary, that is, it costs some producers less than others to produce each loaf of bread. If any producer sells at a price that is less than their unit cost they will incur a loss; so the minimum price at which each producer is willing to sell is their unit cost. Table 3.2 gives the minimum price of each producer in our model.

Unit cost
The cost of producing one unit of that good.

TABLE 3.2   Producers' minimum prices

Producer	Minimum price
ABC	45p
Bakelite	49p
Crusty	56p
DeliLoaf	60p
Easybread	64p

Similarly, consumers differ both in how much they have to spend and how much they like bread, so they will have different *maximum* prices that they are willing to pay for a loaf of bread. If a loaf costs more than their maximum price they will use their money to buy something else. Such maximum prices show the value each consumer puts on a loaf of bread. Table 3.3 gives the maximum price each consumer is willing to pay in our model.

TABLE 3.3   Consumers' maximum prices

Consumer	Maximum price
Alex	70p
Brian	64p
Craig	58p
Damien	53p
Edward	49p

We now make another simplification and assume that each producer only sells at most one loaf and each consumer buys at most one loaf. Again this simplification should make the model easier to understand while retaining the main features of the process under investigation.

Producers make a surplus (a profit) from the difference between the price at which they sell their loaf and the unit cost of the loaf:

Profit   =   Price – Unit cost   = **Producer's surplus**

Similarly, each consumer wants to buy their loaf at a low price to save money that could then be spent on other goods. The money that each consumer 'saves' is the difference between the price actually paid for the loaf and the maximum price that the consumer would have been willing to pay for it:

'Saving'= Maximum price – Price = **Consumer's surplus**

Both producers and consumers are interested in making their surpluses, profits and savings respectively, as large as possible.

4.1   Stage 1: No market

In order to understand what markets do to prices, it is useful to start by assuming that there is no market and instead a benevolent authority decides who will sell to whom. The authority does this by matching up all producers and consumers and fixing the price at which each pair deals, so that the producer sells at a profit and the consumer makes some 'saving' over the maximum price they would have been prepared to pay. In other words, all producers and consumers receive some surplus.

Producer's surplus
The difference between the price at which a producer sells a good and its unit cost of production.

Consumer's surplus
The difference between the maximum price the consumer would pay for a good and the actual price at which it is bought.

The outcome is represented in Table 3.4, in which each row represents a deal. The first row reports on Deal number 1. In this deal, the producer, ABC, sells a loaf to the consumer, Edward, for 47p (the price of the deal). We chose 47p because it is half-way between the minimum the producer would sell at, its unit cost (45p), and the maximum price the consumer would pay (49p), but we could have chosen any figure between 49p and 45p.

The producer's surplus (profit for ABC) is:

$$\text{Price of the deal} - \text{Unit cost} = 47p - 45p = 2p$$

The consumer's surplus (Edward's saving) is:

$$\text{Maximum price} - \text{Price of the deal} = 49p - 47p = 2p$$

The second row of Table 3.4 gives the same information for the deal between the producer Bakelite and the consumer Damien, who trade at 51p (column 6). The producer's surplus is calculated by subtracting its unit cost (column 3) from the price (column 6) and the consumer's surplus by subtracting the price (column 6) from the maximum price he would have been prepared to pay (column 5).

TABLE 3.4   Outcome of transactions under a benevolent authority

Deal number	Producer	Unit cost	Consumer	Max price	Price of the deal	Producer surplus (profit)	Consumer surplus (saving)
(1)	(2)	(3)	(4)	(5)	(6)	(7)	(8)
1	ABC	45p	Edward	49p	47p	2p	2p
2	Bakelite	49p	Damien	53p	51p	2p	2p
3	Crusty	56p	Craig	58p	57p		
4	DeliLoaf	60p	Brian	64p	62p		
5	Easybread	64p	Alex	70p	67p		
Total							

ACTIVITY 3.3

Calculate the remaining producers and consumers in a similar way and fill in the rest of columns 7 and 8 of the table. Then fill in the total producers' and consumers' surplus. (Answers are given at the end of the chapter.)

COMMENT

You should find that the outcome has the following characteristics:

- every producer and every consumer has made a deal with a positive surplus; nobody is excluded

- the deals are made at different prices ranging from 47p to 67p (column 6)
- the total surplus is 20p, which is found by adding the sum of total profit, 10p, from column 7, to total consumers' 'savings', also 10p, from column 8.

4.2   Stage 2: Introducing the market

Now, let's consider what happens if we start to introduce a market by letting buyers and sellers choose with whom to trade and at what price.

Agents could choose to trade with the same partner with whom they traded before under the benevolent authority (Stage 1 of the model). However, this is not very likely. ABC, the most efficient producer with the lowest unit costs (45p), knows that it has received the lowest price (47p) among all producers and that it can do a lot better. It will look for another consumer who is willing to pay more, such as Brian or Alex, whose maximum prices (64p and 70p respectively) are higher than Edward's (49p). Although it received a higher price than ABC, Bakelite also feels it could do better.

Similar considerations apply to consumers. Alex and Brian, who are paying high prices to inefficient producers, would do better by buying from producers who would accept lower prices. Would you choose to buy a product from an expensive store, when you can find exactly the same product cheaper somewhere else?

The following day, therefore, Alex trades with Bakelite and Brian trades with ABC at prices they can agree on, somewhere between the minimum the producers will accept and the maximum the consumers are willing to pay. Alex and Bakelite trade at, say, 54p, while Brian and ABC trade at 59p, prices that are an improvement from both the producers' and consumers' points of view. Alex and Brian are paying less than they paid before while Bakelite and ABC are receiving higher prices than previously. If Craig and Crusty stick to trading together, what will happen to DeliLoaf, Easybread, Edward and Damien, who were the trading partners of the four agents (Alex, Brian, ABC and Bakelite) that now trade together? We know that DeliLoaf is very inefficient – its unit costs, 60p, are among the highest. So DeliLoaf cannot trade profitably with Damien or Edward, both of whom have a maximum price (53p and 49p respectively) that is lower than DeliLoaf's unit costs. The same applies to Easybread, whose unit costs, 64p, are even higher than DeliLoaf's.

DeliLoaf and Easybread are also excluded from the market because they cannot sell at a profit. Similarly Damien and Edward don't buy bread and spend their money elsewhere.

Table 3.5 summarizes the outcome of this second stage.

TABLE 3.5   Outcome of transactions: beginnings of a market

Deal number	Producer	Unit cost	Consumer	Max price	Price of the deal	Producer surplus (profit)	Consumer surplus (saving)
(1)	(2)	(3)	(4)	(5)	(6)	(7)	(8)
1	ABC	45p	Brian	64p	59p		
2	Bakelite	49p	Alex	70p	54p		
3	Crusty	56p	Craig	58p	57p		
Total							

ACTIVITY 3.4

Complete Columns 7 and 8 of Table 3.5.

(Answers are given at end of this chapter.)

COMMENT

The completed table shows the following:

- Only three deals have occurred and four agents have been left out of the market.

- The range of prices has reduced considerably; they now vary from 54p to 59p, with a range of only 5p, while before they varied from 47p to 67p, a range of 20p. This is because the exclusion of DeliLoaf and Easybread, who needed high prices to be profitable, and Damien and Edward, who needed low prices to be willing to buy, has reduced the range of possible prices.

- From the last row of the table we can see that the total surplus is substantially larger now than before (20p+22p=42p rather than 20p) despite only three deals having been carried out instead of five. This is a result of the range of prices being reduced and both inefficient producers and consumers who value the good less than others being excluded from trading.

4.3 Stage 3: Equilibrium prices

However, some agents feel there is still scope for improvement. Brian and Craig, who have paid 59p and 57p respectively, would prefer to buy bread at 54p, which is the price that Alex paid. On the other hand, Bakelite and Crusty, who sold at 54p and 57p would make more profit charging 59p, which is what ABC sold at. *While prices are different, agents know there is always scope for improvement.* This is competition in the market. Producers and consumers keep looking for new trading partners and better prices until all trades occur at one single price.

So, prices tend to become more and more equal until they converge on a single price. When there is a single price, the market is in equilibrium because no agent has any incentive to change what they are doing. Table 3.6 shows the results when everyone trades at the same equilibrium price.

TABLE 3.6   Outcome of transactions with an equilibrium prices

Deal number	Producer	Unit cost	Consumer	Max price	Price of the deal	Producer surplus (profit)	Consumer surplus (saving)
(1)	(2)	(3)	(4)	(5)	(6)	(7)	(8)
1	ABC	45p	Brian	64p	57p	12p	7p
2	Bakelite	49p	Alex	70p	57p	8p	13p
3	Crusty	56p	Craig	58p	57p	1p	1p
Total						21p	21p

C O M M E N T

The completed table shows the following:

- The total surplus in the market is the same as in the previous case. The total surplus has not changed because the same six agents are trading, although at different prices. No further increases have resulted from inefficient producers or consumers who do not value bread enough being excluded from the market. This is a limitation caused by the simplicity of this model. With more agents and more stages, further increases in the total surplus would have been possible.

- The process of convergence towards the equilibrium price happened through the interaction of agents looking to increase their individual surplus. It is as though the market was an invisible hand that guided these self-interested agents to maximize the total surplus available.

This is a model for which there is some empirical support. In experimental situations with artificial markets, prices do tend to converge rather quickly to a single equilibrium value. In the economy we find that in many markets where goods are homogeneous (that is, there are no significant differences in quality or appearance) the prices charged by sellers are so close that it is hardly worth shopping around; the market does it for you.

4.4 A market with multiple sales

This is as far as we can get with this model in this form. However, we can learn some more if we relax the assumption that each firm can only sell one loaf to one consumer. This is a usual step in building models; having learned what we can from a particularly simple one, we see what happens if we complicate the model just a little. By allowing firms to sell more than one loaf, we are introducing a more realistic form of competition into the model.

If firms can sell more than one loaf and can sell to more than one consumer, the most efficient firm, ABC, will be able to undercut the prices offered by all other firms. In order to do this ABC must charge a price at which all other firms would make a loss; this price is at most 48p, since at 49p Bakelite can break even. Provided the price is not higher than their maximum price, all consumers will buy a loaf; at a price of 49p or less, this would include Damien and Edward who had previously dropped out of the market. Let's suppose ABC chooses to set the price at 48p to make as much profit as it can while excluding all its competitors.

TABLE 3.7 Results of market transactions with multiple sales

Deal number	Producer	Unit cost	Consumer	Max price	Price of the deal	Producer surplus (profit)	Consumer surplus (saving)
(1)	(2)	(3)	(4)	(5)	(6)	(7)	(8)
1	ABC	45p	Alex	70p	48p		
2	ABC	45p	Brian	64p	48p		
3	ABC	45p	Craig	58p	48p		
4	ABC	45p	Damien	53p	48p		
5	ABC	45p	Edward	49p	48p		
Total							

ACTIVITY 3.5

Complete Columns 7 and 8 of Table 3.7.

(Answers are given at end of this chapter.)

COMMENT

The completed table shows the following:

- The equilibrium price has fallen drastically (from 57p to 48p) because of competition between firms. As a result of the competitive process only the most efficient firm is producing and it has to sell at a fairly low price in order for other firms not to steal its customers. The new equilibrium price is above the unit cost of the most efficient firm but below that of any less efficient firm.

- No other firms are included in the market: ABC sells all 5 loaves that are traded.

- All consumers are included now that the price is lower – however, if there were consumers that had a maximum price below 45p they would be still excluded, even if ABC dropped the price as low as it could, given that its unit cost is 45p.

- The number of loaves ABC can sell depends on how many consumers are willing to pay this price. This means that consumers govern how many loaves are produced. This is an aspect of what is called consumer sovereignty.

- As a result of competition between firms, the total surplus has risen considerably (from 42p to 69p). The surplus mainly goes to consumers because any firm has to keep its price low to exclude competitors.

In this model we had just one producer who was more efficient than all the rest; this producer was therefore a monopolist, that is, the only seller in the market. But this is not a necessary feature. If we extended the model further and had more producers, each of whom could sell as many loaves as they liked, the most efficient producers could undercut all the less efficient producers. Competition between them would drive the price down to just above the unit costs of the most efficient producers. This would whittle the producers' surplus away and boost the consumers' surplus. So where there is competition between producers, consumers make all the gains.

SUMMARY

The model shows that when self-interested producers and consumers are free to choose their trading partner, producers seek consumers who are willing to pay high prices and consumers seek producers who are willing to accept low prices. We can make some general points about such a market process.

- Consumers who are not willing to pay much for the good, either because they have low incomes or do not like the good much, and inefficient producers who cannot sell at a low price are excluded.

- The range of prices at which deals take place tends to become narrower over time until prices converge towards a single equilibrium price.

- Such convergence happens as a consequence of economic agents pursuing their own interests; no external authority co-ordinates the market. This is an example of Smith's 'invisible hand' in action; it requires no benevolence or concern for others on the part of economic agents to achieve a co-ordinated outcome.

- As prices converge towards the equilibrium price, the total surplus increases as inefficient producers and consumers who are not willing to pay as much for the good are excluded from the market.

- Competition between producers favours consumers since they gain the benefits of being able to buy from the most efficient producers. Consumers decide what is produced and in what quantity through their actions in the market; how much of the good is produced depends on how much consumers value it. This is an aspect of what's been called 'consumer sovereignty'.

- Not all consumers are equally 'sovereign' in the market: their influence depends on how much money they have to spend.

5 EXTERNALITIES AND THE 'INVISIBLE ELBOW'

The neoclassical model of the market outlined in Section 4 seems to provide a strong rationale for leaving the allocation of resources to markets. The model shows that competition ensures that markets are efficient so that resources are used in the way that best reflects consumers' values. So we can say that, on the one hand, markets are social structures in which the pressure of competition constrains the behaviour of economic agents. On the other hand, the model emphasizes the scope for agency that consumers have in the market, because of the freedom and sovereignty that the market process gives them.

So if we as consumers care about the environment, the market should listen to us. If the environment is not protected in a market economy, perhaps it is because consumers do not value it enough or because the ones who do value it have too little money to spend – after all, environmentally friendly goods are sold in the market. Is the problem simply that we do not value the environment sufficiently – we don't put our money where our mouth is – or is there something missing in this 'invisible hand' model of how markets work that matters when we use it for looking at the environment? Are natural resources in some way different from the type of commodities that we have been using so far to illustrate how markets work?

5.1 Externalities

As we noted earlier, environmental damage is usually an unintended consequence of actions taken for quite different reasons. This is because the effects of environmental damage are typically experienced by people other than those who cause it. In a market economy, decisions about the use of resources are left to individual economic agents, who will, in general, decide what to do on the basis of the **private costs and benefits** to themselves, rather than by considering the wider global effects of their actions on society as a whole – the **social costs and benefits**. Private costs have to be paid for; a firm has to pay its labour force, buy raw materials, invest in machinery, etc. However, a decision to produce something may also cause social costs, costs for others, for example, through damaging the environment. As these are costs that the decision makers do not have to pay, they are unlikely to take them into account when deciding what to do.

Private costs and benefits
The private costs and benefits of a market transaction are those costs and benefits incurred by the buyers and sellers involved in the transaction.

Social costs and benefits
The social costs and benefits of a market transaction include, in addition to private costs and benefits, those costs and benefits incurred by other agents not involved in the transaction.

"It may be industrial effluent to you lad—but it's a new Bentley and a heated swimming pool to me."

The 'responsibility' for environmental degradation does not only lie with producers. Consumers who buy from them will also pay less than the full cost of the products they consume. When we decide to buy food produced using pesticides because it is cheaper than organic food, we pay a price that reflects only the private costs of producing it, and we let society as a whole foot the bill for the difference between the social and the private costs. When private and social costs diverge, the market allows environmental damage to be caused as the unintended consequences of the exercise of consumer choice and the pursuit of profit by producers. In such cases, we say that there is an **externality**, because some of the cost is external to the decision makers.

Externalities can be positive or negative. The flowers we grow in our gardens for our own enjoyment may also give pleasure to our neighbours; this is a positive externality. Most environmental problems, however, arise from negative externalities, where producers or consumers do not bear the full social costs of their own decisions. This is most obvious when waste is

Externality
Externalities occur when private costs and benefits differ from social costs and benefits. In such cases, economic agents do not pay the full costs or enjoy the full benefits of their action.

dumped elsewhere, as in the acid rain produced by the industry of one country falling on another. But it is also true when those who cause the problem are not the only people who experience it, as in the cases of fish stocks being depleted or smoke polluting the atmosphere. In these cases the environmental damage is a cost to everyone, but if only the cost to themselves is taken into account by decision makers, this will be much less than the full social cost.

FIGURE 3.4   Forest killed by acid rain, Poland

An economic system that depends on the market to co-ordinate individual decisions is prone to externalities and the environmental problems these produce. We can examine how these are caused and some of the remedies proposed, by looking at the three different types of environmental problems we mentioned in the introduction to this chapter.

5.1.1   Exhaustible resources

Many of the world's natural resources, such as forests and fish stocks, can become exhausted if not used judiciously. If anyone can make use of them there is always a tendency for them to be overused. The problem here is that the full costs of overfishing, for example, are not borne by the individuals who do it. Overfishing causes costs for others; these are negative externalities. Individuals who catch fish gain income from selling it. However, if this catch reduces subsequent fishing opportunities, this imposes costs on everyone who might fish in the future. These costs will get passed on to the future customers who will have to pay higher prices. In this case the individuals who fish bear only a part of the total social costs of their fishing. Further, an environmentally conscious individual reducing his or her catch wouldn't help. Unless everyone reduces their catch, any individual who reduced his or her catch will lose income from having less fish to sell, but still suffer the consequences of everyone else's overfishing. Without any other form of co-ordination, market forces give each individual a powerful incentive to catch as many fish as possible.

One solution that has been suggested by some economists in such a case is to make sure exhaustible resources are privately owned. If the seas were privately owned and their owners charged others for fishing in them, the owners would look after the fish stocks because they would be concerned about losing fishing revenues in the future; if the fish stocks were running out, they would not be able to charge so much for fishing. Overfishing would be a cost to the owners. In other words, what are currently the external costs of fishing would become private costs to the owners. To cover these costs, the owners would charge a fee for fishing that reflected the full social cost; there would no longer be any externalities. So it could be argued that in the case of exhaustible resources the problem of externalities is caused by the fact that the market is missing. Markets need property rights in order to work; if nobody owns a resource, the incentives of the market are missing. The solution to such externalities and the environmental problems they cause is to introduce the market by granting property rights over all exhaustible resources.

The problem, however, with this solution is that it is not clear that a private owner would necessarily take into account all social costs in the way you or I would want. Think of a forest, for example, although it might be in the interest of private owners to ensure their future income and restrict logging by charging for it, there is no guarantee that they will choose to do so in such a way that will preserve or replenish the forest. It might turn out to be in their interest to flatten it and develop housing on it. All private ownership does is privatize the costs of overuse, but some other externalities, such as those due to the effects on the level of carbon dioxide from cutting down the forests, may still arise. Further, the forest owners may have different priorities than you or I, and if the sums don't work out for them in favour of preserving the forest, the market will not save it.

FIGURE 3.5
Surui Indian children watch a logging road being cut through their reservation in the Amazon

An alternative solution would be to put it into social ownership, with society managing the resource and charging for or controlling its use in other ways. The buying and selling of fishing quotas allocated by the European Union is an example of this. National or supra-national control is not the only form social ownership can take; traditionally, many societies managed to preserve their natural resources through social norms controlling their use. However, the encroachment of the market on people's lives frequently breaks down such traditional norms.

5.1.2 Public goods

It is not always possible to allocate property rights in a common resource. Certain common resources, such as clean air, are known as **public goods**. For such goods, it is not possible to exclude others from their consumption. For example, we all breathe the same air. This means that even if people value it, the market cannot provide clean air. If someone wanted to pay to have cleaner air for herself, she could only do this by paying for everyone to have cleaner air. She would not be able to recoup any of her expenses because others, known as 'free riders', could not be prevented from using the cleaner air that she had paid for. If everyone benefits, whether or not they pay, why should anyone pay?

> **Public goods:**
> These are goods (such as air) for which it is impossible to exclude others from consumption, and the consumption of which does not reduce the total amount available.

So in the case of public goods, the externalities that arise from their being held in common cannot be avoided by establishing private property rights. Even if we wanted to, we could not create private ownership of a public good such as the air; it would be meaningless since an owner could not stop everyone else using it. In this case the only solution would be social ownership. In a market economy this would mean a payment to people who created or improved public goods and a charge, or tax, on those who despoiled them. This is the idea behind 'green taxes' which make polluters pay the costs of the damage they cause. This corrects, or at least reduces, the externality.

5.1.3 Future generations

The third type of environmental problem referred to in the introduction involved the interests of future generations being hurt by the actions of people alive today. In this case, the problem is that the social costs that impact only in the future may be nobody's current private costs; today's activities can cause big negative externalities for future generations. Consumers influence the outcome of markets only through the money they have to spend. The interests of future generations are ignored by the market because they have no purchasing power. There may be some ways in which the interests of future generations are represented indirectly, for example by current parents, but even with the best of intentions they are likely to put less value on the future than their children would. To anyone alive today, the quality of air we breathe today will matter at least as much if not more than the quality of the air in the year 2100, but to children born in 2099 only the latter will matter.

Again there appears to be very limited market solutions to this problem. Various political solutions have been suggested including appointing guardians to look after the interest of future generations. But such guardians can only work by going against the market; the market in itself cannot properly look after the interests of people not yet born.

5.2 The 'invisible hand' and the 'invisible elbow'

As we saw in Section 2, one of the strengths of the market is that it co-ordinates the decisions of individual consumers and producers, without any of them needing to take account of what others are doing. Each simply had to know the prices at which he could buy and sell goods in order to decide what to do. Further, the outcome brought general prosperity, even though each participant looked only to his own interest. However, in this section we have seen how, in the context of externalities, this same characteristic, that people do not need to take account of what others are doing, is the market's weakness. People need have no idea of the environmental damage their economic decisions may be causing. Consumers, even if they care about the environment, are not informed by the market about the environmental impact of the products they buy. Nor, indeed, are producers informed about costs they impose on others, unless they are required to pay for them. So the environmental impact of market transactions is typically inadvertent.

This happens because, in markets, agents make their decisions solely on the basis of prices. The failure of markets to care for the environment suggests that, if we are concerned with preserving the environment, the information summarized in the price of goods is incomplete. The price mechanism that we have explored in our model is good at maximizing the total monetary surplus in a market, but it fails to deal with other issues that might be important, such as environmental degradation or ethical issues. When we buy a good because it is cheaper we don't know whether the only reason it is cheaper is, for example, because it has been produced by a more polluting technology or by using child labour.

The environmentalist Michael Jacobs talks about this phenomenon as the 'invisible elbow' of market forces, saying that a counterpart to 'the "invisible hand" which Adam Smith argued brought general prosperity... can equally be an "invisible elbow" which brings general ruin. ... often elbows are not used deliberately at all; they knock things over inadvertently' (Jacobs, 1991, p.25).

SUMMARY

- Environmental problems are often caused by externalities that occur when agents do not have to pay all the costs of their actions.

- Where there are externalities, private and social costs differ. Where social costs are greater than private costs, agents may carry out actions that they would not have carried out if they had to pay all the cost of their actions.

- Externalities lie behind the environmental problems that occur when exhaustible resources are depleted, when public goods are spoiled and when future generations have to pay the cost of current actions.

- Policies to overcome the problems caused by such externalities include putting exhaustible resources in private ownership and making agents pay the full costs of their actions through imposing green taxes.

- A market economy is inherently prone to externalities because economic agents make their decisions on the basis of price alone and do not necessarily know or care about external costs. In a market economy, externalities function like an 'invisible elbow' that inadvertently knocks over those things that are not accounted for by the 'invisible hand'.

6 CONTROLLING THE 'INVISIBLE ELBOW'

We have just seen that market economies are prone to externalities, because the price mechanism does not provide agents with all the information about the wider consequences of their actions, and people are not encouraged to consider interests other than their own. Moreover, even if people were informed and environmentally concerned, market forces may leave them no room for manoeuvre. Competition forces producers to cut costs wherever they can to survive – this will include off-loading costs through externalities wherever possible, especially if their competitors are already doing so.

So what can be done to have the benefits of the 'invisible hand' co-ordinating the market but keep the 'invisible elbow' under control? Two types of market solutions were proposed in the previous section: extending private ownership by assigning property rights, and green taxes and subsidies to bring private costs in line with social costs. However, these market solutions pose some problems that arise from distributional issues, usually from the fact that existing resources are not equally distributed among economic agents.

The solution based on assigning property rights immediately begs the question to whom should such rights be assigned? In practice, in past 'privatizations' of this kind, such as the enclosure movement in England, those who were better off were allocated the bigger share of the previously common land. But even if property rights are equally divided among the population with a claim on a resource, the outcome in the long run is still likely to favour the rich. This is for two reasons. First, the free use of resources held in common, such as common land, is likely to have made more difference to the living standards of the poor than to those of the rich. So even if the poor gain as much as the rich from privatization, they lose more in comparison with the past. Second, markets have a tendency to concentrate resources. Private property can be sold for money, and money is more likely to be needed urgently by the poor than by the rich. So for one reason or another, a bad harvest perhaps, poor people are more likely to end up reducing their holdings, and rich people are more likely to be able to expand theirs by buying other's shares.

Externalities also have distributional implications because they are costs imposed by one agent on others. There won't be only one way to correct that externality and each way will have specific distributional effects. In particular, externalities can be corrected by providing either carrots or sticks. For example, the government could either subsidize farmers using an environmentally friendly way of controlling pests or tax those who use environmentally dangerous pesticides. A green subsidy is just like a negative green tax; it too can be used to correct a difference between social costs and private costs, to encourage environmentally friendly actions where private costs are too high.

6.1 Power in the market

A significant problem with making the market work better is that it will reflect some people's wishes more than others; some consumers are more 'sovereign' than others.

As you saw in Section 2, when resources such as coffee become scarce, the price will rise and people who are prepared to pay more for their coffee will continue to drink it; those not prepared to pay as much will switch to other drinks. The total quantity of coffee produced will be determined by a myriad of such decisions about how much each individual is prepared to pay for a cup of coffee. If what you are prepared to pay also depends on your income, the influence of people with more income will be greater than that of poorer people in determining, for example, how much coffee is produced, how much oil is extracted, how much pollution is allowed.

This problem of unequal power is a feature of the way markets work. Markets give power to people in accordance with the money they have to spend. This is because the only way to make needs and wishes felt through the market is to be prepared to pay for them, in order to turn those wishes into 'effective demand' or spending power. How much one's wishes can be put in the form of effective demand will depend on how much money one has to spend rather than the importance of those wishes in any objective sense. A peasant village that is unable to raise the few hundred dollars needed to have a water pump in their village will have a much less effective claim on their own local water supply than consumers in the west who are spending thousands of dollars on buying out-of-season vegetables that depend on water from the same source.

Richer people may be able to avoid the effects of environmental degradation more easily than poorer people, by paying more for their fish, by buying bottled water or by buying houses in lower risk environments. This means that they may have less stake in avoiding environmental degradation than poorer people. But the rich have more power in the market place and so the market solution will take more account of their views. The answer that the market comes up with about the 'right' amount of environmental degradation may not be one with which the poor agree. It is only 'right' in the sense that the market balances the effective demands of rich and poor and this is a very unequal contest.

The people with the least effective demand are those that have no money at all. These include most children alive today and all generations not yet born. They have no way of turning their wishes into direct effective demand. Instead they have to rely on others doing it for them, but the fact that children are more likely to live in poverty than adults in all countries (except in a few Northern European welfare states) suggests that relying on other people does not often lead to equitable outcomes. This also means that concerns about the condition in which we are leaving the planet for future generations are unlikely to be addressed by a market solution.

6.2 The problems of valuing the environment

Green taxes and subsidies also pose the question of the level at which they should be set. Ideally they should be set at a level that makes the private costs of any activity equal to its social costs. But how can those costs be assessed? Where the costs are borne by profit-making firms there may be a way of measuring the profits lost as a result of a specific polluting activity. But what about the costs to the population more widely and to future generations?

One way to measure such costs is to ask people how much they would be prepared to pay not to have the pollution or, alternatively, how much they would need to be paid to put up with it. However, again there are distributional issues raised by this. Rich people might be able to pay more not to suffer from the effects of pollution and might need to be paid more to agree to put up with it than poorer people could or would. Does this mean that polluters should be taxed more highly for polluting areas in which rich people live? If this was the case then polluting firms would locate in poorer parts of the world. This relocation can also happen because richer countries have felt able to impose tougher environmental regulations on firms than poorer countries. This is because the revenues that such firms bring is needed more by poorer countries than richer ones. Not surprisingly, the worst polluting industries are located in the poorest parts of the world.

Finally there is the issue of how we measure the cost that environmental problems will impose on future generations. They cannot be asked how much they would pay not to have such problems, so we have to find an answer by imagining ourselves in their position. Another problem then arises of how to value what happens in future years compared with what happens today. Most people alive today would argue that the compensation needed to persuade them to accept pollution today would be more than that needed to accept pollution to be suffered in ten years' time, and much greater than for pollution to be suffered in one hundred years' time. But members of future generations will not think like this, since the effects of pollution suffered today are no problem to them.

6.3 Beyond the market

Finally some things that are lost through environmental degradation may be impossible to value. How can you put a value on the beauty of the countryside? It doesn't just mean the loss of a resource. You may never make use of the countryside, but you can still appreciate its existence and care that it continues not only for your own or your children's enjoyment but also for the community more widely. The neoclassical model that you examined in Section 2 worked on the assumption that all wants could be satisfied by the consumption of goods and services. If that was the case then we *could* put a value on them. But other wants and needs cannot be analysed in the same way as a desire for consumption goods.

Similarly, in the neoclassical model all resources are privately owned. The neoclassical solution is to make the world like their model and make sure all material resources are privately owned. We might have other reasons for not wanting to extend private ownership. We may put a positive value on living in a society in which the mountains and the seashore belong to us all, rather than one in which property rights are parcelled out.

Finally, the neoclassical model works on the assumption that everyone acts according to their self-interest and builds its picture of the economy on this basis. But perhaps in reality it is the other way around. Perhaps it is living in a market economy that makes people act in their own self-interest and lose any sense of responsibility for the effects of their actions on the environment. As social scientists, we need to recognize that people behave differently in

"We do our best here to build a better world for the next generation – of nuclear reactors, that is."

different sorts of society. If we lived in a more environmentally friendly society, one in which people cared more about each other and therefore about the environment, externalities might not be the problem that they are today.

SUMMARY

- All market solutions to environmental problems have distributional implications. They will hurt some people and favour others. In particular, assigning property rights may deprive poorer people of access to common resources that they depend on more than richer people. Further, markets tend to concentrate privately held resources thus increasing income inequality.

- Market solutions to environmental problems might also not be fair because people who are wealthier have a greater power in decisions that are taken 'by the market'. It is not the number of people affected, but the money that can be spent on something that matters.

- How to value the environment in order to set green taxes or subsidies is not a straightforward technical issue, it is open to much political debate, especially when the interests of future generations are involved.

- The market model assumes that people's desires to own and consume material things is more important than anything else, but it is possible that people value other things, such as the nature of the society in which they live.

- Instead of markets being the solution, they may be part of the problem. It may be living in a market economy that makes people not know, not care or not be able to do anything about the effects of their actions on the environment.

7 CONCLUSION

• •

This chapter has given you a flavour of the debates about the effects of economic activity on environmental degradation, especially focusing on market economies. In doing so, we introduced a simplified model that focused on the price mechanism, as a way of understanding markets. We learnt about the power of the price mechanism, but also its limitations, especially as far as environmental degradation is concerned. We saw how the existence of externalities in markets can make the simplicity of the price mechanism dangerous for the environment. Market prices provide neither information nor the incentives needed for agents to make decisions that take the environment into consideration.

We briefly examined possible corrections to the market that could help limit environmental degradation, such as the introduction of property rights to combat the excessive exploitation of exhaustible resources and green taxes and subsidies. We also saw that distributional issues are not only about who gains and loses from such policies but also about the power that individuals have in the market; those who have more money will have more say in the outcomes that result. This will not always reflect the value that other, poorer people may put on the environment.

We also saw that the neoclassical approach assumes that people are concerned only about their own interests and that these interests can be reduced to the ownership and consumption of material goods. But people may care about other issues, such as the type of society in which they live and the natural environment that surrounds them. Further, the type of society in which people live may affect whether and how people care about the environment.

REFERENCES

Maddison, A. (1991) *Dynamic Forces in Capitalist Development: A Long-run Comparative View,* Oxford, Oxford University Press.

Maddison, A. (1995) *Monitoring the World Economy, 1820-1992,* Paris, Development Centre Study of the OECD.

Jacobs, M. (1991) *The Green Economy,* London, Pluto Press.

Smith, A. (1776) *An Inquiry into the Nature and Causes of the Wealth of Nations* 1971 edn, eds Campbell, R.H. and Skinner, A.S., Oxford, Clarendon Press.

FURTHER READING

Bowers, J. (1997) *Sustainability and Economics: An Alternative Text,* London, Longman – a critique of neoclassical environmental economics for students of economics. The author is both an economist and an environmental campaigner.

Andre Gorz (1994) *Capitalism, Socialism, Ecology,* London, Verso – a socialist view on the relationship between politics, economics and the environment.

Michael Jacobs (1991) *The Green Economy,* London, Pluto Press – a very clear account of a whole range of economic positions on the environment, from a perspective critical of the neoclassical orthodoxy.

David Pearce (1993) *Economic Values and the Natural World,* London, Earthscan Publications – a clear but occasionally slightly technical account of the neoclassical position.

Peter Saunders (1995) *Capitalism: A Social Audit,* Buckingham, Open University Press – an enthusiastic view of how the neoclassical model can make capitalism and environmentalism work together.

Schumacher, F. (1973) *Small is Beautiful: Economics as if People Really Mattered,* London, Abacus – a classic and pioneering work of environmental thought written for the general reader.

ANSWER TO ACTIVITY 3.3

The completed table should look like this:

Deal number	Producer	Unit cost	Consumer	Max price	Price of the deal	Producer surplus (profit)	Consumer surplus (saving)
(1)	(2)	(3)	(4)	(5)	(6)	(7)	(8)
1	ABC	45p	Edward	49p	47p	2p	2p
2	Bakelite	49p	Damien	53p	51p	2p	2p
3	Crusty	56p	Craig	58p	57p	1p	1p
4	DeliLoaf	60p	Brian	64p	62p	2p	2p
5	Easybread	64p	Alex	70p	67p	3p	3p
Total						10p	10p

ANSWER TO ACTIVITY 3.4

The completed table should look like this:

Deal number	Producer	Unit cost	Consumer	Max price	Price of the deal	Producer surplus (profit)	Consumer surplus (saving)
(1)	(2)	(3)	(4)	(5)	(6)	(7)	(8)
1	ABC	45p	Brian	64p	59p	14p	5p
2	Bakelite	49p	Alex	70p	54p	5p	16p
3	Crusty	56p	Craig	58p	57p	1p	1p
Total						20p	22p

ANSWER TO ACTIVITY 3.5

The completed table should look like this:

Deal number	Producer	Unit cost	Consumer	Max price	Price of the deal	Producer surplus (profit)	Consumer surplus (saving)
(1)	(2)	(3)	(4)	(5)	(6)	(7)	(8)
1	ABC	45p	Alex	70p	48p	3p	22p
2	ABC	45p	Brian	64p	48p	3p	16p
3	ABC	45p	Craig	58p	48p	3p	10p
4	ABC	45p	Damien	53p	48p	3p	5p
5	ABC	45p	Edward	49p	48p	3p	1p
Total						15p	54p

Living with risk: the unnatural geography of environmental crises

Steve Hinchliffe

chapter 4

Contents

1 INTRODUCTION

Throughout this book you have repeatedly been asked to question the idea that nature and society exist as separate categories. So, in Chapter 1, what we call human nature was shown to be the result of complex interactions between what we have been used to calling social and natural matters. The implication was that if we fail to recognize the importance of these interactions we end up with a limited understanding of what it can mean to be human and of complex human experiences, as diverse, and seemingly natural as sexuality and death. Likewise, you read in Chapter 2 that a person's health is a product of a mixture of social conditions, bodily matters and environmental quality. Failing to take account of one or more of these may well reduce the effectiveness with which we can deal with ill health. Finally, in Chapter 3 you read that our lives are bound up with market practices. Arguably, there is no place on the planet that isn't touched in some way by markets. If we fail to take account of the ways in which markets work then we will miss an awful lot of the current means by which nature and society are being mixed together and churned up on a daily basis.

After reading the previous chapters you may be thinking that nature and society are now so thoroughly mixed together that it makes little sense to use the terms at all. In all of the examples it is very difficult to identify where society stops and nature starts, and vice versa. One things is for sure, the diagram used in the book Introduction to represent purified notions of the social and the natural depicts a mode of understanding that is of very little use in helping us to understand the issues that have been raised in this book. You might like to experiment with alternative diagrams as you read on. In any case, we will come back to the diagram in the Afterword to this book.

Now, given this mixed up state of affairs, we can ask a number of questions. These are the central questions for this chapter. You should write them down and aim to answer them as you work through the chapter:

1 If society and nature are no more than two sides of the same coin, why do we often talk as if they are separate matters?

2 What do we gain and what do we lose by holding nature and society apart like this in our thoughts?

3 Can we carry on for much longer thinking that society and nature are essentially amenable to separation?

These may seem to be rather abstract questions. This is not something that is necessarily foreign to social science. Nevertheless, social scientists do often seek to develop their ideas with reference to specific issues. They look to particular instances and for evidence. These may help to support their ideas or may end up challenging them. Either way, social science is often a matter of being involved in the world, asking questions of it and allowing it to ask questions of you. To this end, we can develop some answers to the three questions by focusing upon particular themes and issues. The theme for this chapter is environmental **risk**. The issues are natural hazards and food scares.

We start, in Section 2, by looking at natural hazards, concentrating in particular on extreme weather events. With an eye on question 1 (above), I will ask just how natural are natural hazards and why is it that we describe them as natural in the first place? We shall then compare two risk events, one that was described as a largely social affair and one that was attributed to nature. The comparison will help to offer some answers to question 2. In Section 3 the focus shifts to food production and consumption. The risks associated with food manage to bring society and inner and outer natures together in ways that are often arresting. We shall look in particular at the 'mad cow' or BSE (Bovine Spongiform Encephalopathy) crisis that developed in Britain in the 1980s and 1990s. The aim will be to use this case to develop some further thoughts on question 2 and to open up answers to question 3.

In sum, the aim of this chapter is to investigate environmental risk by highlighting the ways in which the two poles of nature and society become entangled as we look more closely at threats and hazards. In addition, the argument will be made that part of our current predicament with regard to environmental risks is that we tend to view the world as made up of bits of society and bits of nature. Once we start to collapse these distinctions we may be in a better position to live more effectively with risk.

Risk
Exposure to dangers, adverse conditions and threats. To take a risk is to know that an action may prove costly. The magnitude of the risks may be relatively well known (in the form of a probability), or they may be largely unpredictable.

2   THE UNNATURAL GEOGRAPHY OF NATURAL HAZARDS

● ●

The one thing that you can always rely on in Britain is the unreliability of the weather. In 1998, the British climate seemed to have been unusually unreliable. And the damage was immense (particularly for the people who lived in areas of storm damage or flooding). At the start of the year, 'freak' windstorms tore off roofs in Selsey Bill. At the end of the year, storm-driven waves battered the coastline to such an extent that parts of Beachy Head, near Eastbourne, crumbled into the sea. The weather-beaten British Isles seemed to be caving in, physically, and in the case of the white,

FIGURE 4.1   A weather-beaten coastal town – Tynemouth, north-east England

chalk cliffs of south-east England, symbolically. Easter, 1998, saw large parts of England and Wales under water. Five people died as a result of the floods. Over 4,000 properties were flooded. In autumn, the floods returned. People started to look for someone or something to blame. People wanted to know the cause of all this damage and disruption to the established order. In the distant past, accidents were blamed on the gods, a God or some other supernatural entity. Today we tend to look for new scapegoats or 'non-caused causes' (see Box 4.1). In Section 2.1, we shall look at who or what gets the blame for such events. Sections 2.2 and 2.3 then discuss who or what benefits from the ways in which we explain such hazards and risks.

BOX 4.1	**Acts of God to acts of El Niño – a cause without a cause, a new scapegoat?**

El Niño is a name used to describe the warm oceanic and atmospheric conditions that can occur along the western coast of Ecuador and Peru. The term initially referred to the annual shift in ocean currents that brings warm weather around the end of December (El Niño means 'baby' in Spanish and refers to the events surrounding the nativity in the Christian calendar). El Niño now more generally refers to an unusually intense occurrence of this annual shift which brings even warmer atmospheric and oceanic conditions. These unusual events occur every three to seven years.

El Niño has been a topic of conversation in Peru, Ecuador and Chile for centuries, as it tends to disrupt the availability of fish in the region. Now meteorologists argue that the change in air and ocean temperatures can not only disrupt the weather and economy locally, its can also have effects across the entire Pacific region and even further afield.

El Niño became the prime suspect for many of the world's ills in 1998. From strange weather to economic instability, almost everything was being linked to the shift in ocean currents. The media exposure given to El Niño was so great in the United States that there was a report that a man named Al Nino, who lived in Texas, was receiving telephone calls lambasting him for all the havoc he was causing.

Without underestimating the physical power of El Niño, it is easy to see it as a convenient scapegoat. El Niño was thought to be a natural process, for which nothing else was to blame. The convenience is that this type of non-caused cause gets everyone else off the hook (except poor Al Nino). So-called 'natural' phenomena like El Niño are useful because they provide the means for downplaying human complicity in world events.

Unfortunately, El Niño may soon lose its status as a non-caused cause. The possible causes of El Niño are themselves now under scrutiny. Some meteorologists are arguing that human-induced climate changes are contributing to the increased frequency and intensity of the baby. It may no longer be so easy to deny human complicity in world events. Or we may simply need another scapegoat.

2.1   Who or what gets the blame for natural hazards?

The clue to answering this question is in the name – natural hazards. We can take an example to see how this blame game pans out. The extract in the following Activity is an attempt to pin the blame on to something. It was written by employees of the Environment Agency, an organization responsible for, amongst other things, flood defences and the issuing of flood warnings in England and Wales. It might be useful to note that, after the Easter floods in England and Wales in 1998, a finger of suspicion was being pointed at the Agency for certain alleged failures of responsibility. The details of the account are not important. What is important is the attempt that is being made to identify the causes for the flooding.

ACTIVITY 4.1

As you read the extract in Reading 4.1, note down who or what is being blamed for the floods. Who is being exonerated?

Preliminary report on the Easter floods, Environment Agency, April 1998

So far, April 1998 is the wettest April for 100 years and is likely to be the wettest since records began. Most rain fell between 8 and 19 April. During Wednesday 8 April and Thursday 9 April an area of unstable air met an area of rising air associated with a weather front. Heavy thundery showers occurred in the unstable air along the front. The combination of these two processes led to the very high rainfall totals observed over a short period of time [...]. The Met Office forecast for Easter – 'cold with rain, heavy at times' – grossly underestimated the actual rainfall.

and

Exceptionally heavy rain fell on parts of Wales and Central England over Easter, causing widespread flooding. Initial estimates indicate over 4,200 properties were flooded from surface water run-off or rivers overtopping banks or flood defences and spilling into the flood plain. Flood defences in many of the hardest hit areas, such as Northampton and Banbury, were not designed for floods of the magnitude seen over Easter, which might be expected to occur perhaps once in every 100 to 150 years. Tragically, 5 people were drowned or died as a result of the floods. This could have been far worse, but for the excellent response of the emergency services.

Source: Bye and Horner, 1998, p.16

This is a technical document, but it is also full of issues that are of interest to social scientists. Indeed, the writers of this report are doing a form of social science. It is perhaps important to note that people who call themselves social scientists aren't the only ones doing social science. This is especially the case if you think of social science as a form of investigation, and the social scientist as somebody who resembles a detective or criminal lawyer. Of course, this is not the only or even the best way of describing social science practice, and I don't want to suggest that we all need to imagine ourselves as TV-style detectives. Nevertheless, social science work often involves sorting through a mass of evidence – numerical data, conversations, gestures, written texts, pictures and so on – with the aim of interpreting these materials in order to arrive at an account which offers some form of explanation for the events or phenomena that interest or concern us. The account will normally be accountable to the evidence that we use to construct it (in this way, social scientists often think of themselves as different from writers of fiction, although they can use similar literary devices to very good effect in constructing their accounts, making arguments and so on).

Now, the Environment Agency's preliminary report on the floods in 1998 is a particular kind of account. Its aim is to find a cause or set of causes for the event under investigation. And it is doing a specific kind of job. It is trying to sort through the evidence in order to assign responsibility to various actors in the flood protection system. And it is doing this by *making a fairly clear distinction between social agents on the one hand, and natural agents on the other.*

The most obvious culprit, as far as the Agency is concerned, is the weather. The report argues that a set of unusual atmospheric conditions produced a period and intensity of rainfall for which no-one could have realistically been prepared. Indeed, it suggests that flood defences (for which, remember, the Agency is responsible) are designed to cope with a certain level of river discharge. There is a practical limit to flood protection schemes – any higher and they would be far too expensive and would interfere too much in the normal hydrology of the system. Meanwhile, apart from blaming the freak weather conditions, there is a suggestion that the meteorologists underestimated the rainfall in their forecast. They failed to understand the weather in sufficient detail. This meant that the flood defences and emergency procedures were not as well primed and prepared as they might have been. Of course, the meteorologist would soon defend herself by arguing that there are limits to which a complex, chaotic weather system can be truly known. Again, blame would be shifted on to the weather itself (or perhaps on to El Niño).

Why do you think 'nature' is often blamed for hazards of this kind? Might it be a way of shifting responsibility on to something that can't answer back? Is it a means of hiding human complicity in the production of a disaster? (You may want to return to Box 4.1 to consolidate your views on these questions.)

It is now worth focusing in more detail on the kind of explanation that is being offered. As we have seen, when things go wrong, the search is on for someone or something to blame. In the language that has come to characterize social science, we look for an agent, normally a person or an organization, sometimes a non-human. The agent is someone who or something that we believe has shaped the events that we want to explain. They are, in this version of social science explanation, the prime cause (or prime suspect).

As far as the Environment Agency were concerned, the 1998 floods in England and Wales were to be explained through a 'natural' cause (the weather). This form of explanation is represented in Figure 4.2. Notice how, in this version of events, nature is seen as the cause of society moving from an ordered state to a disordered state.

Notice also that in this form of explanation, nature and society are seen as largely separate categories. Nature visits disorder upon society. This account of the flood presupposes a *purified* view of nature and society (see Figure 1 in the book Introduction). Meanwhile, the form of explanation assumes that there is a clean break between a condition of social order (before the flood)

A 'normal' scene in Northampton

The same street after the flood

FIGURE 4.2   The form of explanation used to account for natural disasters

and social disorder (after the flood). Now, in one sense this is self-evident – and if your home or street were flooded you would agree whole-heartedly as you set about cleaning up, or restoring order. But, it takes more than heavy rainfall to produce a flood. The water is not the only guilty party. For one thing, there needs to be something there to flood. Perhaps planning regulations were too lax or were ignored so that building could take place in areas that were liable to flood. Or we could say that the system of land use was part of the cause of the flood. Too many trees have been removed, too many smooth surfaces have accompanied urbanization, too many farmers have ploughed up hedgerows, too many rivers have been straightened, too many roads, drains and sewers have been built. All of these activities can speed up the movement of water into the rivers and so can lead to a rapid and intense build-up of river discharge. If this happens, the river is unlikely to be able to cope and so bursts its banks. In this case, the flood is not the fault of nature (or even the weather), it is the specific mix of the natural and the social that is under suspicion. The hazard has emerged from the 'interactions between people and environments' (Mitchell *et al.*, 1989, p.405). It is not simply an external event visited upon a blameless social order.

FIGURE 4.3   Some land-use changes have tended to increase the rate at which rainwater reaches a river, so increasing the likelihood of flooding

So, rather than seeing disorder being imposed on society, we could argue that the disorder is already there, lurking in the social and natural landscape, well before the actual 'event' or 'disaster'. It is contained within the daily lives of people. The flood could be viewed as an accident waiting to happen, in which case blame has to be distributed more widely. Blame can't rest on the event itself. Causes (like the agricultural system, or, ironically, the over-abstraction of water from rivers and groundwater) will be found before as well as during the flood.

So who or what was to blame? As social scientists we should be suspicious of any attempt to pinpoint any one particular cause, or attribute this to any one particular person or other entity. We are not setting out to find a scapegoat to replace the supernatural (or for that matter the natural). We are not looking for another creature that we can pin the blame upon and hope, rather like the animals that were accused of all manner of crimes in medieval trials, that no-one will care enough about the suspect to question our own motives for assigning responsibility in this way. Instead, it is possible for social scientists to think in more complex ways. We can, as has been suggested throughout this book, begin *to understand the social and the natural as complex, interactive and interrelated matters.*

So where does this leave us? It suggests that we are not looking for absolute causes in social science. Rather, we are interested in a broader understanding of affairs. But this can sound as if social science has no ethics, as if it is missing the tools for deciding that something is right or something is wrong. We can't identify guilty parties from the flow of social and natural activity. Just as we can't blame the weather for floods, likewise we can't blame the regulatory agency (in this case the Environment Agency) because both are operating within a complex world, within which they are partly structured by events beyond their own control. For example, the weather is often not held to be responsible for itself (it is caught up in social activity, as reports of an enhanced greenhouse effect have made clear). Meanwhile, the Environment Agency is caught up in other social worlds (the regulatory system's relationship to the private sector, the willingness or otherwise of people to trust experts and so on) and so-called natural worlds (there *was* a high level of rainfall). Farmers who strip out woodland and hedgerows may be acting in ways that are more or less dictated by the market arrangements that they find themselves in. Indeed, it could seem as though every potentially responsible agent that we identify, upon further analysis, slips from our grasp. They can all claim to be partially determined by the structures within which they are operating. Even El Niño cannot so easily be held to be the prime cause of the floods (see Box 4.1).

This problem can make social scientists very unpopular when they are asked to comment upon a particular problem. It can all too easily sound as though they irresponsibly refuse to find a single cause for something, and thereby end up blaming everything, and ultimately nothing. But before despairing we can try another approach. While realizing that social science is (necessarily) weak at identifying simple causes, it is nevertheless a powerful approach to providing critical interventions that can quickly identify and nullify forms of explanation that are overly simplistic. In this sense, we can be critical, especially when we can spot the 'escape attempts' of those people who may well be at least partially implicated in a matter. In other words, we can use a social science sensitivity to spot inappropriate explanations and suggest that there are social commitments to the accounts that are being offered. So when the buck is being passed, we can be vigilant. In Section 2.2, we shall see how such vigilance can yield a number of insights into the ways in which people and organizations explain and deal with risks and hazards.

FIGURE 4.4   Passing the buck – social scientists can be more vigilant than Steve Bell's policeman

SUMMARY

- In answer to question 1 in the Introduction to this chapter, nature and society are treated as separate in part because there is a tendency to look for simple causes to explain events like hazards. Nature is a favourite scapegoat. It has become the modern equivalent of the 'act of God' explanation for a disaster.

- Natural hazards have social as well as natural causes. They are not external events visited upon people by nature; they emerge from natural and social interactions.

- Social scientists do not always need to look for simple causes. Evidence often points to a more complex picture. Causes are often manifold rather than singular. Social scientists can work with, rather than ignore, such complexity.

2.2 Who benefits from conventional explanations of natural hazards?

The previous subsection established that natural hazards were not simply natural. This statement is underlined as soon as we look to see who and what tend to suffer most after so-called natural disasters. By far the greatest number of deaths associated with natural disasters occurs in those parts of the world where there are profound levels of poverty. This may come as no surprise. Disasters have uneven impacts partly because some locations are more vulnerable than others. Even in the same region, town or village, there are differences in terms of **vulnerability** and impacts.

The poorest, oldest and youngest are often the most vulnerable. In The United States, for example, there is growing evidence that hazard vulnerability divides along lines of race as well as class. Meanwhile, there is evidence that it is women and children who bear the greatest burden of environmental threats in many countries (see **Woodward, 2004** for an exposition of these social categories). This is not to suggest that, in talking of vulnerability, we need to assume that certain groups of people, or other living beings, are somehow helpless victims. These patterns of vulnerability are broad, and there are always exceptions where people, plants and animals cope and even flourish despite the odds. Similarly, there is suffering in places where we would not expect vulnerability.

Vulnerability
Attributes of persons, communities and environments that can increase the potential for suffering from a particular danger or hazardous event.

The point that natural hazards affect those who are most vulnerable is central to the case that hazards are socially as well as naturally produced. In this section, we will be exploring why it is that explanations of events that rely solely upon nature as the cause can benefit some groups, and can work to the disadvantage of others. In addition, I will argue that in order to provide alternative explanations of natural hazards we need to look beyond the event itself. We can think about looking beyond a specific event in two, related ways:

1   **Events have histories**. We can look back in time and ask how is it that the people, the land and the environment become so vulnerable? Has there

been mismanagement of resources? Have planning regulations been ignored? Are gender inequalities producing vulnerabilities?

2   **Events have geographies**. We can look at the interactions that are particular to the place where the disaster occurs, and at the interactions that link one place to other places. Is the economic vulnerability of an area produced in part as a result of unfair trade conditions? Has the area been poorly treated by national and international government? Are there firms operating in the area that are neglecting to invest in the essential services that would reduce vulnerability? Are powerful actors actively containing economic and social risks in a specific place?

We can now explore how it is that natural explanations of natural hazards are beneficial to some people and organizations and detrimental to others. Doing so will highlight the uneven distribution of risks and how it is that vulnerability is produced historically and geographically. We shall compare two risk events that occurred within a month of one another.

2.3   Let them eat bananas – the uneven geographies of risk

A tale of two catastrophes

CRISIS IN WALL STREET: A hedge fund totters and the West organises a $3.5bn rescue package

CRISIS IN CENTRAL AMERICA: At least 11,000 dead, millions are homeless and the West organises a $100m rescue package

Traders on Wall Street buying and selling shares in September (left) while two-year old Felix Silva cries at a shelter for evacuees in Nicaragua this week after the disastrous mudslide

FIGURE 4.5   Front-page headline from *The Guardian*, 7 November 1998

The headline in Figure 4.5 reports on two events that occurred in the latter half of 1998. Both can be described as risk events. The response of Western governments was markedly different for the two cases. As the headline indicates, the first situation led to a massive injection of money from wealthy Western banks and government reserves. The second produced a much more modest, some would say derisory, response from the world's wealthier nations.

Here are two ways of accounting for both of these risk events.

2.3.1 Markets and vulnerability

In the previous chapter, you will have appreciated how markets work through the price mechanism. The market model demonstrated that as markets develop there tend to be winners and losers. There is a period of obvious instability as producers go out of business and consumers look for alternatives. Even when markets are well developed, the price mechanism is such that many of the producers and consumers will be operating perilously close to their break-even point. So markets are means of organizing production and consumption in ways that leave economic agents with little room for error. Markets may look to be stable and in equilibrium, but it doesn't take much to throw the whole game into potential chaos.

Given this understanding of markets, we could argue that both of the risk events in Figure 4.5 were generated through market-produced vulnerabilities. The Wall Street crisis was the result of the instability of emerging financial markets in the previously state-planned economies of Eastern Europe and the former Soviet Union. In the run-up to this crisis, financial speculators in New York, London, Tokyo and elsewhere had invested large sums of money into developing markets in these and other so-called emerging economies. The money came from trusts, endowments, shares and pension funds raised in economically wealthy countries (from private pensions, mortgage endowments, individual savings accounts, unit trusts and so on). The assumption was that such funds would produce sizeable profits that could be returned to the companies, share and pension holders in the future. However, market instability made these funds severely vulnerable.

Following the same logic, we could also argue that the Central American crisis was the outcome of the long-term action of worldwide markets for food products like bananas and coffee. Again, it was companies from the world's more powerful economies (especially from the United States) that had large investments in plantations. Following the market model discussed in Chapter 3, we could argue that the markets had produced a particularly vulnerable configuration of nature and society – so much so that the countries of Central America were unprepared for Hurricane Mitch.

Core and periphery
A model used to express the ways in which economic and other forms of power tend to become concentrated in certain places (the core) at the expense of other places (the periphery).

Both events were in part a result of the worldwide financial system. In this respect they had similar histories and geographies. They both involved movements of money between the financial **core** and the financial **periphery** of the world's markets. So why did the two events produce very different reactions from the financial centres in New York? If they were both the result of market failures, why did only one of the events generate a significant rescue package? To understand this we need to mention some of the institutions that surround markets. This brings us to our second take on these risk events.

2.3.2   Uneven vulnerability through risk management

If the production of vulnerability was driven by similar market arrangements that shared similar geographies linking the core and the periphery of the financial system, then the outcomes of those vulnerabilities were very different in terms of their geography. In short, the banking crisis was in danger of spreading like wildfire down the intricate economic networks that link the money in your pocket to stock transactions many thousands of miles away. The Central American crisis was more contained. It looked as though it would have little or no economic effect on most other parts of the world. To understand the wildly divergent responses to these crises, it is useful to consider in some more detail how these two risk events had very different geographies.

The risk returns – dousing down the fire

As the scale of the banking crisis became apparent, a sizeable tranche of Western government money was mobilized in order to bring about some stability and save the financial system. The reasons for such drastic action are worthy of consideration. In one sense the action was taken because the risks had returned to the 'core' of the financial system. And this would have far-reaching repercussions. Not only were the big banks and moneylenders worried, various people in Belfast, Burnley, Elgin, and Aberystwyth may well also have been concerned. In particular, those people who had invested in pensions or other funds, and were soon going to cash those in, were concerned that their financial arrangements might no longer turn out to be what they may have hoped. So the risks had spread out from unstable markets in Russia and elsewhere. They had not been contained. There was a 'boomerang effect'. The fund managers had become caught up and caught out in their own risk-taking venture. Without the kind of action that was taken by the banks and governments, financial insecurity and heightened risk were about to spread like wildfire. Instability would have hit an astonishing number of governments, companies and households. Bear this wildfire geography of risk in mind as we look at the second disaster.

The risk is contained – let the fire burn itself out

In the aftermath of Hurricane Mitch, the devastation in parts of Central America was almost unimaginable. In Honduras alone, upwards of 7,000 people lost their lives. The estimated cost of repairing the damage ran to several billions of dollars. The affected countries of Central America needed to mobilize large amounts of money in order to avert further disasters including disease and total economic collapse.

Now, following the argument that disasters have histories and geographies, we might expect that those partly responsible for the production of vulnerability would be implicated. In the financial crisis discussed above, the venture capitalists were forced to recognize some of their culpability in the production of financial insecurity. They were part of the process that had produced vulnerability and so their own fortunes were locked into the fate of their ventures. However, in the aftermath of Hurricane Mitch, some of the potentially responsible parties squeezed their way out of the situation, seemingly unscathed by the whole affair. This left others to carry the can.

The risk did not spread out in anything like the fashion it had done for the financial crisis. People in Elgin could still buy reasonably priced bananas. Part of the reason for this was that Western interests, in the form of companies operating in the affected states, were rather well protected. And these companies could divert their operations elsewhere with relative ease. In doing so, they managed their risk effectively by spreading their production across a number of countries and by making sure that they were adequately insured. Of course, this ability to cope with risk was not shared by all parties concerned. For example, in La Lima, a small northern town of Honduras, the banana plantations that provided a considerable portion of the region's income were buried in mudslides or had been irreparably damaged by floodwater. The crop was destroyed. The plantations would take at least three years to recover. One might think that the large US-owned corporations who control much of the banana trade in this part of Central America would be similarly devastated by the disaster. But, as we have seen, vulnerability to disaster is an uneven matter. In fact, the corporations were insured under an 'act of God' clause. As long as the cause of the disaster was seen as supernatural or natural (or any non-caused cause), their losses would be recovered. The plantation workers were not insured. Furthermore, there is evidence that some of them were soon suspended or laid off by the corporations, who were trying to reduce their costs even further (Davison, 1998). In other words, a different geography of risk from the one that affected the financial institutions was taking shape in the aftermath of Hurricane Mitch. The risk could be contained in Central America. Corporations were powerful enough to shift their investments and responsibilities. They could effectively minimize their risk. This containment and the resulting lack of drastic remedial action served to intensify the danger and vulnerability within Central America.

Partly as a result of this successful risk management and partly as a result of the denial of liabilities that became possible when events were described as natural, the response to the crisis in terms of immediate financial aid was paltry. This was especially the case when compared with the response to the September banking crisis. Even worse, no provision was made to reduce or suspend the debt repayments that the countries of Central America were liable to pay to Western banks. The estimated cost of repayments for Nicaragua and Honduras was £1 million per day. Several development and aid agencies made the metaphorical link between the deaths caused by drowning in the floods and mudslides, and the deaths that were caused by the drowning of the economies of these countries in debt repayments.

ACTIVITY 4.2

Now answer the following questions. You may find it useful to refer back to Sections 2.2 and 2.3 in order to develop your answers:

1   In the aftermath of Hurricane Mitch, who benefited from conventional explanations of natural disasters?

2   How do companies and others manage to avoid risk?

3   Make a list of who or what contributed to the Hurricane Mitch disaster and a separate list of who or what suffered the worst effects. What do these lists tell us about the geographies of vulnerability?

COMMENT

1   In the Hurricane Mitch example, the beneficiaries are fairly clear. The large, multinational companies and the debt financiers can both absolve themselves from responsibility for the production of vulnerability. Companies may even turn the disaster to their advantage as they can use it as an excuse to trim their workforce. The attribution of the disaster to natural forces is clearly a way that can be used to obscure the geography and history of vulnerability production. It is a way of de-socializing and therefore depoliticizing the event.

2   The economic risks taken by the corporations in Central America were relatively well controlled. They managed to shift their production interests to other regions, were insured and were able to terminate labour contracts with relative ease. In short, they had made sure that nothing would bind them to the region if things became too unstable. All this careful risk management served to intensify the risks faced by plantation workers.

3   The geography of vulnerability production and the geography of vulnerability are very different. If the crisis in Central America was

produced by many people and organizations over a long period of time and across many countries, then the effects of the crisis were felt by a concentrated group of people in a handful of countries. Figures 4.6(a) and 4.6(b) on pages 134 and 135 are a schematic mapping of the contributions and suffering that can be associated with the disaster.

We have reached the half-way stage in this chapter. Our task so far has been to look at the ways in which natural hazards are explained, and this has suggested some of the ways in which our explanations can contribute to the uneven characteristics of risk. Arguments have also been made about the ways in which social science works. By refusing to accept simple explanations, especially those that load causal responsibility on to 'nature', we have started to produce different takes on the world. As you read the following summary points, you might like to refer back to the first two of the three questions that were posed in the introduction to this chapter.

SUMMARY

- Explanations of natural hazards tend to play down human complicity in an event.

- Calling something natural implies that it is non-social and therefore inevitable, unchangeable and non-political.

- Not only is nature a scapegoat that allows people to cope with the uncertainties of everyday life, but potentially culpable agents benefit from having matters described as natural. It can be a means to shift responsibility away from themselves.

- A social science alternative is to look for the geographies and histories of events, highlighting the interrelations of nature and society – in that way we can start to argue that things are not always inevitable. They might have been, or can be, otherwise.

Our task is now to look at risks and risk taking in some more detail.

FIGURE 4.6(a)   The production of vulnerability. The diagram represents schematically some of the financial and commodity linkages and connections between the region of Central America and other parts of the world. If the region becomes vulnerable, then these links, along which money and goods will flow, are part of the explanation for the risks

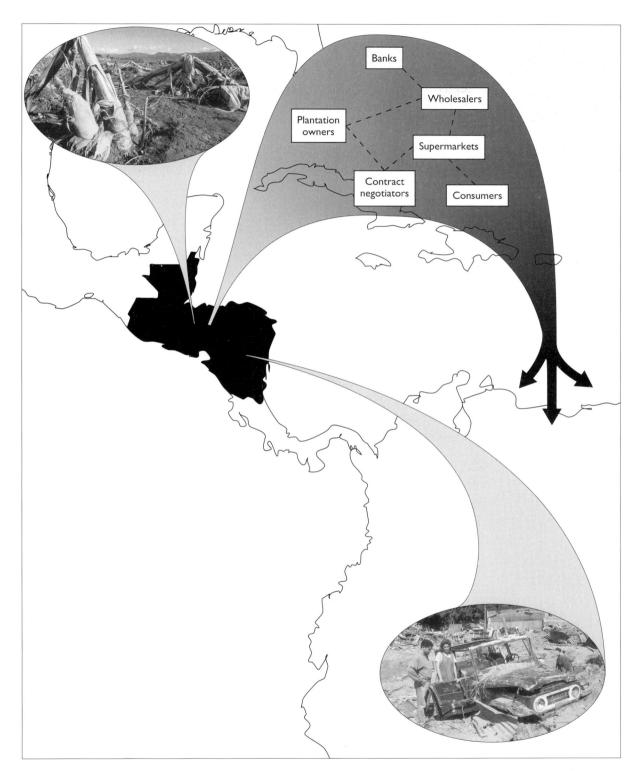

FIGURE 4.6(b)   The containment of risk. After the hurricane strikes, some of the contributors to the risk situation are able to extract themselves from the scene. The actions of the plantation owners, other large corporations, supermarkets and so on may mean that consumers in places like Britain need never know that there has been a disaster. The effect in Central America is to increase vulnerability

3 LIVING RISKY LIVES – EATING OUTER NATURE

The workers in Honduras, the plantation owners, the large produce corporations, the fund managers, the banks, governments, mortgage holders and pension contributors, despite all their differences, shared a common characteristic. They all lived with risk. For some social scientists, living with risk has become one of the defining characteristics of our modern, or what some call late modern, times. That is not to say that social scientists would argue that people live riskier lives today than they did in the past. Such an argument would be too general and would not reflect the diversity of risk experiences that we saw in Section 2 of this chapter. So when the German sociologist Ulrich Beck argued, in the late 1980s, that we now live in a **risk society**, he was not making a general case that life was somehow more dangerous today than it was in the past (his argument was published in English in 1992). Rather, the claim was that there had been a qualitative shift in the ways in which people live with risk, and that this shift had occurred, in the main, in the latter half of the twentieth century.

Risk society
An account of modern society emphasizing shifts in the ways in which risk awareness, uncertainty, dependency and trust developed in the twentieth century.

We can summarize these shifts as follows (adapted from Macnaghten and Urry, 1997, p.254):

1   Public awareness of the riskiness of hitherto mundane aspects of daily life has intensified.

2   There has been a growth in the degree of uncertainty that surrounds those risks.

3   People's sense of dependency upon the institutions and expertise responsible for managing and controlling risks has grown.

4   At the same time, the degree of public trust in those institutions and in expertise to manage risks effectively has diminished.

Putting these points together, we can say that in a risk society there is a tendency for debate and contestation over matters that were previously taken for granted or were formerly matters of general agreement. (Think of the various, co-existing conceptions of health that you were introduced to in Chapter 2 as a manifestation of this proliferation of information and argument.) In order to have those debates and to make decisions that were hitherto less likely to be faced as choices, we need more and more information and knowledge. The irony, if it can be called that, is that we need all this knowledge just at a time when many people have started to lose their beliefs and trust. Institutions like organized religion, the family, science, business and government are arguably no longer held in the esteem that they may have once enjoyed. In a risk society, none of these institutions is assumed to have a monopoly on the truth.

Our concern in this section is to understand the relevance of nature–society relations to this risk thesis. Our aim, in particular, is to address the third question that was raised in the introduction to this chapter. As a start, it is worth remembering that in the Central American case risk was intensified in the daily lives of many people. And this intensification was produced when large corporations, debt financiers and others sought to deny their role in producing vulnerability and so deny their responsibility to the affected areas. It was suggested that these denials of responsibility were in part made possible by the ability to separate nature from society in the explanations of disaster and hazard. Furthermore, by ignoring the *social-and-natural* causes of the disaster there was a failure to come to grips with the production of vulnerability. And this might have knock-on effects in the future. Lessons will not have been learned, new appropriate structures will not have been put in place. This and other accidents will continue to wait to happen. It might not be long before even the sophisticated risk management of the international corporations and the insurance industry starts to feel the strain.

Perhaps, therefore, one major cost of trying to hold nature and society apart in our thinking and explaining is the production of more rather than less risk? If this is the case, the suggestion is that it is no longer feasible to treat nature and society as anything other than two sides of the same coin.

We shall now explore the risk society and its relation to questions of nature–society interrelations by focusing on the BSE crisis that developed in Britain in the 1980s and 1990s. We start with some background to this crisis.

3.1   Do cows make you mad?

In this book we have tended to make a simple distinction between inner nature (our genes, organs and our bodies) and outer nature (roughly speaking, our environment). There are times when this distinction seems to make sense. Indeed, it may be one of the issues that we take for granted in our daily lives. But there are times when this convenient division is suddenly and spectacularly undermined. At these moments we realize the extent to which our bodies are intricately wrapped up in broader social and natural worlds. One of these moments was the BSE or 'mad cow' crisis.

For some sections of British society, the Sunday joint of beef has been part of a ritual joining together a wholesome self, the nuclear family and the nation. (If you are unsure, think of Beefeaters at the Tower of London and the nickname given to the British people by the French – *les rosbifs*.) For growing children and working men (eating meat has often involved a particular performance of gender), eating beef, and incorporating it into the body, was regarded as an essential part of being morally and physically fit for society. The pure slice of meat was a link between the purity and bounty of the land, the family kitchen and the healthy, working body. To be sure, this comfortable world has been punctured a number of times before. Excessive

FIGURE 4.7 A 'traditional' scene: a family sitting down to Sunday roast beef and trimmings

eating of red meat has been linked to dietary disorders and heart disease for many years. Likewise, there have been many campaigns to raise public awareness of intensive farming and animal suffering, particularly with respect to veal production. So concerns were already in place. But the BSE crisis seemed to bring these and other concerns together. As a result, many commentators have argued that the significance of eating beef – and indeed the public view of the food production industry, science and government – changed substantially in the wake of the crisis.

The desperate images of diseased cows, disoriented, frightened and stumbling across farmyards, tapped into a general concern over modern industrial agriculture. Something was very wrong. This was a moment at which people could no longer so easily forget where their food came from. Beef products did not just come from the supermarket, surrounded by advertising images of contented cows re-enacting a scene from *The Sound of Music*. The beef product had a more complex history and geography, including a countryside and an agricultural system which looked increasingly unlike the idyllic rural images that represented Old England. The intensive rearing of cows, the protein-enriched feed containing rendered animal products, the slaughterhouses and rendering plants that processed animal carcasses at astonishing rates, were matters that were all brought to the public's attention. And they were all matters that many meat-eaters would have preferred not to think about. Indeed, the entire food production system shifted from being taken for granted (and possibly being viewed somewhat romantically) to being a cause for general concern. As it did so, the relationship between inner and outer nature was thrown into relief. At the same time, both of these 'natures' were shown to be unavoidably linked to a huge and profitable industry, replete with competing interests. Beef products had connected nature and society for a long time. After BSE, any public fears regarding these connections were intensified.

FIGURE 4.8   Images of the food industry changed during the BSE crisis – an abattoir worker 'processing' a carcass

At one level there was a simple though crucial question that the government and the public were asking in the late 1980s and 1990s: 'Is beef safe to eat?' The question referred to the possibility that the eating of BSE-infected beef products might induce a new variant of Creutzfeldt-Jakob Disease (CJD – the human equivalent of BSE) in human beings. It also referred to the efforts being made to exclude infected products from the food chain. This matter was by no means straightforward in an industry that was technologically set up to process dead animals at high speed and to use virtually every 'component' of the carcass. BSE was also likely to be carried by animals not showing clinical symptoms. There was no known test that would identify carriers of the disease. Even the initial cause and the identity of the disease carrier or agent were the subject of disagreements. So sorting out infected stock from 'clean' stock, and good meat from bad meat, became huge logistical and practical problems for the industry.

ACTIVITY 4.3

Look back to the four characteristics of a risk society that were set out at the start of Section 3. Concentrating for the moment on the first three points, to what extent do you think the BSE crisis is representative of a risk society issue?

COMMENT

In many ways the BSE crisis seems to provide plenty of evidence for the risk society. We can take each point in turn.

1   Eating beef was once an activity that was largely taken for granted. It was part of a routine, wrapped up in ideas about nationhood, gender, religion and identity. The BSE crisis threatened this comfortable existence. Traditions as well as health now seemed to be at risk. These concerns were not necessarily new. They were, however, undoubtedly intensified during the crisis.

2   The risks associated with eating beef were difficult to judge; no-one knew what was causing the disease. Other uncertainties included: whether or not the disease could jump species and infect human beings; whether or not cows could be diagnosed in time to remove them from the food system; whether the meat industry could adjust its methods to minimize the risk to humans.

3   Dependency upon scientific expertise and upon governmental institutions was pronounced. BSE-infected meat was not something that anyone could detect. It did not smell or look any different from safe beef. Many cows may well have carried the disease without showing symptoms. Scientific expertise was therefore necessary to provide diagnoses and develop knowledge on the causes and effects of the disease. Government was relied upon to provide the right kind of restrictions and policies to manage the crisis. The agricultural system and the food industry were relied upon to implement policies effectively.

We can now look more closely at the fourth characteristic of a risk society, that of declining trust. I will do this by focusing upon how certain prominent experts dealt with the crisis, followed by an assessment of how their pronouncements on the risks of eating beef were treated by the public.

SUMMARY

- A number of sociologists have argued that broad cultural changes have produced a society where risk has become a more prominent issue in people's lives.

- A risk society is characterized by a change in public awareness, a growth in uncertainty, a growth in dependency on experts and a reduction in the level of trust in expertise.

- The BSE crisis involved a qualitative change in people's attitude to food, a high level of uncertainty and an increased sense of dependency upon expert systems and institutions.

3.2 What the experts said

In a risk society it is assumed that people will, initially at least, turn to expert institutions in order to receive assurances or otherwise on a threat or hazard. In this section we look at three 'expert statements'. The aim is to pick out some of the characteristics of expert statements in order that we may understand how they were received (or why some of them were ignored) by the public.

ACTIVITY 4.4

Read the extracts in Reading 4.2. As you read each extract, try to summarize the position that was being taken on the risk of BSE being transmitted to humans. In particular, you should note down:

1 What level of risk was assumed by each of the writers – how safe did they think it was for people to eat beef?

2 How certain were the writers of their risk calculations?

3 Why do you think there are differences between the three statements? Are there any similarities?

The government scientist

Mr Keith Meldrum, Head of the Ministry of Agriculture Veterinary Service, said the risk of the disease being transmitted from cattle to humans could not be completely discounted, but emphasized that it was only a remote possibility. [...] The Government's measures were more than adequate to remove what was 'probably a zero risk' to consumers:

> I am totally content that what we are doing now is totally sound and is all that we need to do in order to remove any possibility of BSE exposure to man [sic] from cattle. However, I cannot say there is no risk to man from BSE. It is too early. We have only had this disease in this country for three years and the incubation period in man in cases of encephalopathies is very long indeed.

Source: Keith Meldrum, Chief Veterinary Officer, Ministry of Agriculture, Fisheries and Food, quoted in *The Times*, 22 January 1990 (also cited at the BSE Inquiry, 19 October 1998)

The government minister

As the chief medical officer has confirmed, British beef can continue to be eaten safely by everyone, adults and children.

We have taken action to deal with the public health concerns and the animal health aspect of BSE on the basis of the best independent scientific advice.

Source: John Gummer, Minister of Agriculture, Fisheries and Food, 18 May 1990, quoted in *The Times* (also cited in Irwin, 1995, pp.21 and 23)

The dissenting scientists

Man [sic] may not be vulnerable. There is no data on which to make a prediction. The best result would be no effect at all; the worst could be the development of Creutzfeldt-Jakob Disease on a massive scale 20–30 years hence. This could be followed by vertical transmission in man. [...] There seems little prospect of these uncertainties being clarified by research over the next few years.

Source: Professor Richard Lacey and Dr Stephen Dealler, June 1990, Report to the UK Parliamentary Agriculture Committee (cited in Lacey, 1994, p.106)

COMMENT

First of all, I will deal with the differences amongst the three statements (including my thoughts on questions 1 and 2) and then follow this by looking at the similarities.

Expert differences

When I looked at the three accounts I was struck that they were all ostensibly talking about the same thing, and yet there were some glaring differences in the ways in which they understood the risks. The government scientist suggested that the risk was so small as not to be worth considering, although there was an admission that he might be wrong. The minister suggested that there was no risk whatsoever, everything was under control. There was no expression of doubt. Finally, the dissenting scientists suggested that the risks were at that time unknowable. There was therefore a chance that the risks were very high. The only thing that they were certain of was that there was currently uncertainty in any future prediction.

The reasons for the differences in the accounts of risk provided by these people can partly be linked to their different social positions. The government minister was concerned that any message expressing doubt or uncertainty, even if it was only a hint that there might be a minute risk, would be seized upon by the press, by consumers and by foreign competitors. He was critical of Keith Meldrum for even mentioning the possibility of risk in press interviews. Both men were under intense pressure from the agricultural lobby and from the Department of Trade and Industry to say the right things in public. British exports were at stake. There was a good deal of money on the line (the export trade in beef was worth roughly £500 million), not to mention Britain's international reputation. So, in this sense, Meldrum and Gummer's statements were fairly similar. They were both of a mind to believe the risk assessments and interpret any residual uncertainties as irrelevant. The difference was that Meldrum felt bound to express a small, residual doubt. He was not only committed to the farming industry, having to represent their interests in his press statements, but he was also bound to the conventions of science. His argument therefore included the cautionary note that all the evidence was not yet available. There were more questions to ask, and more answers to find. Gummer was less impressed by this argument. He was more interested in answers than questions. He had to make decisions on the basis of the 'best independent scientific advice' (he could have added 'currently available', but did not do so – such an admission would have undermined his case). This was his reasoning: there was no scientific evidence that BSE in cattle was reaching human beings through oral consumption; therefore there was no risk.

Lacey and Dealer's reasoning was more akin to Meldrum's than it was to Gummer's. To paraphrase their position: while it was granted that there was no evidence that BSE was reaching human beings through oral consumption or that resulting infection could lead to development of CJD, that was not to say that evidence would not be found in the future. Lacey and Dealer suggested that 'no data' was indicative of the lack of good research in this area and not an excuse for limited action. Whilst they were not aware of any evidence that proved that humans were at risk, they argued that there was also no evidence that humans were *not* at risk. More time and resources were needed to carry out research into this matter. Until then, we should act as if there was a high risk. We needed to act with *precaution*. A **precautionary approach to risk** was justified, they were arguing, because even a small chance of being wrong was still a chance that could lead to a catastrophe. It wasn't right to ignore the chance given these potentially catastrophic circumstances.

Expert similarities

The first similarity that I spotted in the three accounts was that they all referred to science. This is perhaps not surprising. Scientific approaches to risk assessment have traditionally been the preferred policy tool of British government in food and other kinds of risk events. Indeed, when the UK government sought advice on the BSE crisis it relied solely upon scientific opinion and committees made up of medical, veterinary and zoological specialists.

The second similarity is harder to spot. It relates to the understanding of uncertainty. The statements all give the impression that with more science and technology we would progressively remove the uncertainties. That is, *uncertainty and risk were thought of as temporary matters*: with more research any residual doubt would be progressively eliminated. The assumption of all the writers was that scientific evidence would be built up by conducting experiments on laboratory animals in order to understand more about the infectious properties of the disease agent and about the development of the disease in mammals. The risks would not only become known (through ever more sophisticated experiments), they would also become *predictable*. They could then be minimized by applying more technical expertise to the problem. The latter would involve placing new restrictions on farming and food-processing activities. In the BSE case, this

Precautionary approach to risks
Acting with care, especially when there is a lack of agreement on the outcomes of an action. This may involve taking a more expensive action in the short term to reduce the risk of paying a high amount later.

procedure involved experimental feeding trials to determine the infectivity of various parts of a diseased cow. The results of the trials suggested that certain parts of infected cows were more infectious than others. A policy was then formulated which stipulated that various cuts of beef be removed from the food system (so-called 'specified bovine offal', initially including the spine and head of the cow).

In sum, scientific research, combined with better technical management of the food system, allowed successive agriculture ministers and ministry scientists to argue that 'progress' was being made. The main disagreement in terms of the three statements that we have looked at here was about the rate of that progress.

Contrary to the second characteristic of the risk society described at the start of Section 3, we could say that the experts largely thought that any growth in uncertainty around the matter of eating beef was a temporary matter. For these people, modern science and technology could still be relied upon to produce a more certain world. In Section 3.3 we shall see that all parties in the BSE crisis did not necessarily share this faith in science and technology.

SUMMARY

- Experts representing science and government differed in their opinions as to the risk of contracting CJD from British beef.
- The government expressed the risk as zero, partly in an attempt to reduce the public concern and protect the market in beef.
- Scientists continued to express uncertainty, although they disagreed over the relative importance of the uncertainties.
- Despite their differences, government and scientific experts were of the opinion that, in time, the risks could be determined and controlled. Uncertainty was a temporary matter that would be progressively removed with more research and better policies. The government put a good deal of faith in natural science as a means to develop policy.

3.3 Rationalities and cultures of risk

Despite the repeated assurances from government ministers and their scientific advisors that 'in the normal sense of the term' eating beef was 'safe', there remained a high level of discomfort with respect to the risks of eating beef in Britain. Local councils took beef off the menu in schools, and large restaurant and fast food chains made it known that they were sourcing their beef from outside the UK. Many consumers sought out alternatives and beef prices collapsed. Other European countries refused to import British beef, with France holding out the longest, until 2002. The government and its advisors labelled this behaviour as irrational. They accused the public of being misinformed and of not understanding the science (for an account, see Wynne, 1996a). In this section, we shall look more closely at what was labelled as rational and irrational in the crisis. I will argue that the public understanding of the issues was far from being inferior to that of science.

ACTIVITY 4.5

Do you think it is irrational to take some large risks whilst refusing to take what look as though they are much smaller risks? Under what circumstances might you regard this behaviour as entirely reasonable? Compare eating beef with using mobile telephones (with its radiation risk), playing dangerous sports and drinking alcohol.

COMMENT

I will limit my answer to a comparison with mobile telephones. According to the scientific risk assessments, the statistical probability of suffering a radiation-associated illness as a result of using a mobile phone is higher than the risk of developing CJD by eating beef. So why did people buy mobile phones in abundance in the 1990s, while often choosing not to eat beef? One answer is that the benefits of mobile phones may be regarded as far outweighing the potential health risks. People often say that once they have become used to having a mobile phone they feel lost without it. Many people, and many women in particular, feel safer with a mobile phone if they are travelling alone. The more significant risk for them is the physical danger that seems to be partly reduced by being able to stay in touch. So people may *trade off* one risk for another (Wylie, 1998).

In contrast to mobile phone use, people found it fairly straightforward to avoid British beef by choosing alternatives. They could eat chicken, pork, purchase Irish or other beef products, or turn vegetarian. So, even though the risk from eating beef was reportedly very small, it was for many people not worth taking. There is nothing irrational in avoiding minute risk if adjustments to eating habits or behaviour can be made with very little effort or disruption.

How does this sound? Does this reflect your thoughts on Activity 4.5? Is this how you shop? Do you make choices like this, trading risks off, one with another, and considering alternative products? Some people undoubtedly spend a good deal of time deciding how best to spend their money. And there can be little doubt that people do consider health matters seriously. But perhaps we shouldn't be carried away with the idea that a risk society leads to everyone becoming more calculating, making individual, rational choices. Many people feel either that they don't have that much of a choice, or that they buy things and do things without really giving it a second thought. In many ways, the scientific probabilities and risk calculations just don't seem that relevant to people's lives. This brings us to another set of ideas as to why the government's assurances on the safety of beef (and for that matter on genetically-modified foodstuffs or on other issues of the day) were largely ignored. These ideas are less to do with people making individual risk decisions. Instead, they address what might be a called a *cultural shift*.

Earlier I suggested that the crucial question with respect to the BSE crisis was, 'Is beef safe to eat?' The idea that I want to pursue now is that people soon tired of this question – there were too many opinions around to make a useful decision, and people did not have the time to consider all the issues. So the question changed. It became, *'Do we trust these people with the food that we put into our bodies?'*

Structure of feeling
The culture of the period that structures, but is in turn structured by, people's experiences and actions. It is used to take us away from an account of action based on individual agents or on overarching structures.

This question speaks less about individual risk calculations and more about a general **structure of feeling** regarding food, science and government. In particular, the question signals a general discomfort with the risk-assessment culture that informed the way the government handled the risks. This governmental risk culture was based on a rather narrow form of scientific rationality, which saw nature and society as essentially separate matters. The assumption was that scientists could make observations concerning the nature of the disease. These observations could then be turned into knowledge which would be *relevant* to the rest of society. Elsewhere, and outside this governmental risk culture, society and nature were rarely treated as such separable matters. Indeed, many people assessed risk statements (like 'beef is safe to eat') more in terms of who was making the statement than the actual statement itself (for an extended treatment of this argument, see Wynne, 1996b). In other words, people did not make a distinction between a physical risk and the institution that was supposedly in charge of operations. If the latter was found wanting, then people assumed that the risks could get out of hand. In this alternative culture of risk and mistrust, nature and society are regarded as two sides of the same coin. The next subsection focuses on just how the government managed to misjudge this structure of feeling by relying upon a limited sense of (physical or natural) risk.

3.3.1 The reliance on science and the failure to generate trust

Many assessments of risks to human health are based upon animal experiments, 80 per cent of which, in Britain at least, are carried out on mice and rats. There are many ethical considerations connected to animal experiments. These are complex arguments in themselves and cannot be covered in detail in this chapter. However, there are some arguments over the nature of the evidence that such experiments can be expected to produce which can be considered here.

ACTIVITY 4.6

Read the following text which has been used in promotional information produced by the organization Animal Aid. After you have read the text, write a list of reasons why you think that calculations of health risks to humans based on laboratory experiments on animals may result in either incorrect or only approximate human health risk assessments.

> If we relied on laboratory rats, for instance, much medical knowledge would be turned on its head: thalidomide would be considered safe; alcohol would be regarded as no more toxic to the liver than sugar; TB would not be considered a dangerous disease since rats are hardly affected. Smoking would not be held responsible for lung cancer; doctors would reject evidence that oral contraceptives increase the risk of blood clots because in rats they have totally the opposite effect; and we wouldn't consider it necessary to have vitamin C in our diet.
>
> (Summary, from the Animal Aid website (http://www.animalaid.org.uk/), of scientific evidence presented in Sharpe, 1994)

COMMENT _____

When I thought about it, and considered some of the arguments in Chapter 1 of this book on the similarities and differences between and within species, I became increasingly doubtful as to the relevance of the evidence that is produced through animal experimentation. The degree of match between the social and biological lives of small laboratory mammals, kept in cages, usually only for a matter of months, and the lives of over 6 billion human beings seems, at best, approximate. Unlike the laboratory animals, human beings:

- may live long and complex lives;

- are conscious of a range of possibilities and use language to reflect on, and predict, experience;

- will undoubtedly be exposed to all manner of different chemicals, other organisms and physical processes over long periods of time;

- may have particular biological and social characteristics (including allergies, habits like smoking and drinking, experience of pregnancy, and so on).

Your list may contain these and other points. The main issue is that risk assessments based upon laboratory tests are not easily translated to the outside world. Any statement that suggests that the risks that have been determined in a laboratory are equivalent to those that exist elsewhere is itself based on a questionable set of assumptions. At the root of these assumptions is a purified approach to nature and society. The suggestion is that if we can describe the *nature* of a risk then this description will hold whatever the social conditions. Unfortunately, and as has been stressed throughout this book, it is not so straightforward to hold society and nature apart. Any measurement of nature is, in the non-purified world that we have described in this book, a measurement of a particular natural-and-social interrelationship. We can emphasize this point by looking at laboratory science in a little more detail.

Many scientific and technical risk assessments are carried out by simplifying as much as possible of the world in order to concentrate on the processes that cause harm. This is a form of modelling, similar in some senses to the method that you were introduced to in the previous chapter. In order to arrive at a definite answer regarding the hazardous *nature* of a material (like tissue infected with the BSE agent), experimenters try to make sure that no other element of the laboratory environment could cause a reaction or effect. By repeating the experiment with different concentrations of infectious material (or doses), this simplified world also allows the practitioner to identify safe exposure levels. With further analysis, the mechanisms and processes that lead from exposure to illness can be mapped.

Two forms of uncertainty become important when this model of risk is interpreted. *Firstly*, there is always the chance that the knowledge produced in the laboratory may be wrong. Not everything can be controlled and laboratory workers continually have to make difficult interpretations of their results (a slight change in colour, a subtle movement on a screen or a small change in correlation results). Nevertheless, in time, these kinds of uncertainties may well be reduced (but cannot be fully eliminated) as the experiments are repeated. The *second* form of uncertainty arises when this knowledge is used to make predictions about risks in different environments (outside the laboratory). Whilst the risk knowledge in the laboratory may be fairly robust, as soon as we step outside the uncertainties multiply. The experiment is no longer controlled. We are invariably talking about worlds that are infinitely more complex on account of immense natural and social diversity (a point that is emphasized in Activity 4.6).

This radical, or permanent, version of uncertainty does not imply that laboratory or any other form of scientific knowledge is worthless. But it does imply that if knowledge is to be useful, its own limitations must be recognized. Unfortunately, as feminist scholars and sociologists of science have repeatedly pointed out, laboratory science is often confusingly assumed (more often by politicians than scientists) to provide explanations of nature that are applicable everywhere and at all times. Rather than accepting the knowledge produced as a worthwhile explanation of the world under particular (and possibly peculiar) natural and social conditions (those of the laboratory), the knowledge is elevated to being *the* definitive version of affairs. The laboratory model is confused for reality. It is assumed that the model can access a purified version of nature, whereas it more correctly speaks of a simplified set of natural and social interactions.

It is the simplifications that underlie this form of knowledge that become absolutely evident when such knowledge is used to make assurances on risk to the general public. So, when the agriculture minister claimed that he had acted in accordance with the best independent scientific advice, many people were not impressed. Likewise, when these risk assessments of the infectivity of various bovine tissues were used to formulate a strategy of risk management in the food industry, a number of gross assumptions concerning natural and social interrelationships in the food system were made. As Macnaghten and Urry (1997, p.256) describe it, 'Official policy took for granted, *inter alia*, that farmers would comply with official regulations, the abattoir workers would carefully and systematically remove SBO [specified bovine offal] from animal carcasses, and that feed manufacturers would discard mammalian offal in cattle feed.' Given the public understanding of the workings of such a large industry where an international market continually squeezed profit margins, these assumptions seemed at best unlikely and at worst negligent. These kinds of assumptions reinforced a general mistrust of institutions and scientific expertise, especially when the latter were shown to rely upon what people recognized as oversimplifications of social and natural interrelations.

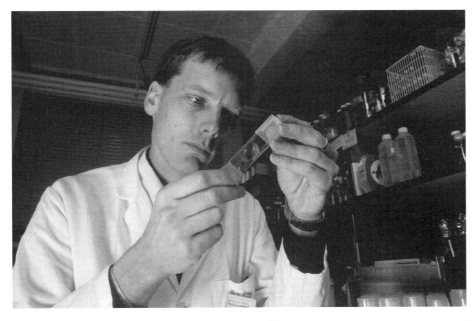

FIGURE 4.9 Science – a practice you can trust?

To be sure, these feelings of mistrust had been around for a long time. Scientists have long been seen, perhaps unfairly, as rather narrow in focus, unable to understand the complexities of social and natural situations (think of the 'bumbling boffin' image that is often portrayed in popular media). Similarly, politicians have long been regarded as capable of being far from independent and getting themselves caught up in various crimes and misdemeanours. But feelings of scepticism were undoubtedly given new impetus during the BSE scare when time and again scientists and government ministers argued that eating beef was safe, only to be faced with growing evidence that their risk calculations and their policies were insufficient. This intensification of mistrust in the general area of food provision continued for some time. So the question shifted from, 'Is beef safe to eat?' to, 'Do we trust government, science and industry with our food?' Furthermore, this was not a question that was asked by every individual as they made decisions on whether or not to eat beef. Rather, the question circulated in the media, in living rooms, in pubs, in schools. It took on a general level of importance. It became part of a structure of feeling. Finally, this structure of feeling would have important effects on the ways in which debates over the acceptability of genetically-modified organisms in food production would be conducted in Britain in the late 1990s and beyond (see **Allen, 2004**). Similarly, the foot and mouth epidemic, which hit the UK and devastated many farms in 2001, was subject to the same structure of feeling, beset by complex disputes and uncertainties.

The BSE example considered in Section 3 is in many ways symptomatic of a risk society. In Section 3.3, I have extended the description of a risk society by highlighting two significant aspects of the BSE crisis:

1   The crisis involved an intensification of mistrust in institutions and expertise.

2   The intensification of mistrust was partly a result of the government's reliance upon a form of logic that treated nature and society as separate matters.

The issue was not that a growth in risk and expert disagreements led to the public losing their trust in science and expertise. The risks of eating meat became less relevant as time went on and the trust was not necessarily there in the first place. Rather, it is evident that the government failed to build up trust by relying upon a form of management that, in neglecting to admit uncertainty where necessary, was alien to most people's experiences and lives.

SUMMARY

- The British government's approach to risk has been to shift responsibility for decision-making on to science. In doing so it failed to recognize the limitations of relying upon a small number of specialized fields of knowledge.

- The government and their scientists interpreted the public's mistrust as irrational and ill-informed, when it is likely that people's everyday understanding of risk was just as sophisticated as theirs, if not more so.

- The rational decision making preferred by the government neglected the permanent forms of uncertainty associated with a diverse natural-and-social world. The government confused laboratory knowledge with natural reality.

- I have argued that laboratory knowledge is a description of a particular set of natural–social interrelations. Its applicability is founded on recognizing these simplifications and not on forgetting that they exist (a forgetting that is accomplished when the science is presented as describing nature and nature alone).

- In dealing with risk, people are less likely to make individual calculations, but rather contribute to a more general culture of trust and mistrust. Social scientists therefore need to think in ways that are not always based upon 'individual' agency. Structure of feeling is one way of bringing structure and agency together in a social science analysis.

4 CONCLUSION

I started this chapter by asking three questions. If you now return to those questions you should be able to offer detailed responses. My comments on the three questions are given below.

1 *If society and nature are no more than two sides of the same coin, why do we often talk as if they are separate matters?*

This question can be answered using the work on natural hazards. Disasters and hazards were shown to be the result of natural-and-social interrelationships. Any description that attempts to purify this mixture by labelling it 'nature' is either a poor description or it is one that is attempting to take someone or something out of the frame of responsibility. Attributing an event to nature can therefore be a political move.

The question can also be answered by referring to the BSE case. One example would be that, by treating the disease as a matter for natural science, the government could refrain from saying anything about the wider issues concerning the morality and sustainability of the intensive industrialization of food.

2 *What do we gain and what do we lose by holding nature and society apart like this in our thoughts?*

As we saw in the Central American case, certain people gain and certain people lose when nature and society are treated as poles apart. More generally, we have argued that the insistence on treating nature and society as separate matters can serve to intensify feelings of risk and feelings of mistrust. The BSE crisis illustrates this matter only too well.

3   *Can we carry on for much longer thinking that society and nature are essentially amenable to separation?*

My answer to this question is, 'Probably not.' The separation of nature and society is starting to cause more problems than it is solving. To be sure, this purified version of the world can help governments make simplifications that can facilitate decision making, but the costs of such simplifications can be profound. Likewise, corporations can benefit from separating nature and society, but if the real causes of disasters like Hurricane Mitch and BSE are thereby not confronted then the gains that are made may only be short-lived. It is for reasons like these that social scientists like Beck and others that you read about in this chapter have called for new forms of decision-making and new institutional frameworks. The next book in this series (**Hughes and Fergusson, 2004**) takes on some of these issues.

REFERENCES

Allen, J. (2004) 'Power: its institutional guises (and disguises)' in *Ordering Lives: Family, Work and Welfare*, London, Routledge/The Open University.

Beck, U. (1992) *Risk Society,* London Sage.

Bye, P. and Horner, M. (1998) *Easter Floods 1998: Preliminary Assessment By The Independent Review Team, Report To The Board Of The Environment Agency*, England, Environment Agency.

Davison, P. (1998) 'No bananas, no homes, little hope', *The Independent*, 15 November, p.16.

Hughes, G. and Ferguson, R. (eds) (2004) *Ordering Lives: Family, Work and Welfare*, London, Routledge/The Open University.

Irwin, A. (1995) *Citizen Science: A Study of People, Expertise And Sustainable Development*, London, Routledge.

Lacey, R. (1994) *Mad Cow Disease,* Jersey, Cypsela.

Mitchell, J.K., Devine N. and Jagger K. (1989) 'A contextual model of natural hazard', *Geographical Review,* vol.79, no.4, pp.391–409.

Macnaghten, P. and Urry, J. (1997) *Contested Natures*, London, Routledge.

Sharpe, R. (1994) *Science on Trial*, Sheffield, Awareness Publishing.

Woodward, K. (ed.) (2004) *Questioning Identity: Gender, Class, Ethnicity*, London, Routledge/The Open University.

Wylie, I. (1998) 'Mad cows and Englishmen' in Ratzan, S. (ed.) *The Mad Cow Crisis: Health And The Public Good*, London, UCL Press.

Wynne, B. (1996a) 'Patronizing Joe public', *Times Higher Education Supplement*, 12 April, p.13.

Wynne, B. (1996b) 'May the sheep safely graze' in Lash, S., Szerszynski, B. and Wynne, B. (eds) *Risk, Environment and Modernity: Towards a New Ecology* (Theory, Culture and Society), London, Sage.

FURTHER READING

Hewitt, K. (1997) *Regions Of Risk: A Geographical Introduction To Disasters*, London, Longman. This provides a thorough review of the hazards research literature in geography and other disciplines. The book is also excellent with respect to the differences between technical and more cultural notions of risk and vulnerability.

Irwin, A. (1995) *Citizen Science: A Study Of People, Expertise And Sustainable Development*, London, Routledge. On risk and science, this provides a thoughtful and clear introduction to the complexities of science and society. The book also makes a useful case for institutional change and more publicly informed modes of decision making in the environmental sphere.

Macnaghten, P. and Urry, J. (1997) *Contested Natures*, London, Routledge. Macnaghten and Urry provide a comprehensive and clearly written book on nature and society issues, including an excellent section on risk society issues.

Ratzan, S. (ed.) (1998) *The Mad Cow Crisis: Health And The Public Good*, London, UCL Press. For those who would like to know more about the BSE case, this volume includes a variety of takes on the crisis.

Afterword

Steve Hinchliffe and Kath Woodward

From our opening examples of cloning and landscapes, to our engagement with human nature, health, economies and environmental risks, we have confronted a social and natural world that looks impure; that is, we have repeatedly found that those aspects of our lives that look to be purely natural turn out, upon closer inspection, to have social dimensions. For example, if we isolated DNA in a test tube, there would be little sign of intelligence. For the latter to be produced we need a complex set of interactions, which would include DNA but would not be reducible to chemical formulae. Our Ryan Giggs clone would not necessarily develop the appropriate experience to become a great footballer. The clone of a recognized intellectual would not necessarily develop the neural connections to become a person of equivalent intellectual stature. Similarly, we have met with situations that we have been used to calling entirely social but which are also dependent upon mixtures of social and natural worlds. The economy, and in particular markets, are good examples of social institutions that result in distributions of goods and services which have implications that are not only social. Markets will tend towards creating a situation where costs are externalized on to zero-priced nature. However, the idea of using nature as a dumping ground for our unwanted by-products in order to save on narrowly defined economic costs has become more and more untenable. The despoiling of land, water and air is starting to have social effects. So we are beginning to realize that we cannot alter nature without having effects upon society. Time and again the modern myth that we can hold society and nature apart starts to falter.

This cross-cutting of society and nature is very different from the purified forms that were referred to in the Introduction to this book (see Figure 1 in the Introduction). Diagrammatically, we have moved from thinking of nature and society as distinct realms or regions to thinking of them as interlaced or entangled. One way of redrawing this figure would be to make the circles overlap. Another, perhaps more graphically interesting, way would be to draw a tangled web or network. No matter which thread you follow, be it social or natural, you will always become entangled in other social and natural networks and threads (see Figure 1).

The initial aim of this book was to demonstrate that nature and society exist in mixes. A second aim was to establish the importance of re-thinking nature and society at a time of increased uncertainty and risk. Our third aim was to demonstrate the skills and resources available to social scientists when confronting nature and society questions. In order to emphasize some of the progress that has been made in the foregoing chapters it will be useful briefly

FIGURE 1 Nature and society entangled

Source: based on Latour, 1993, Figure 4.3.4, p.102

to consider three social science themes that have informed the writing of the chapters of this book. The themes are, structure and agency, uncertainty and diversity, knowledge and knowing.

Structure and agency

The theme of structure and agency runs throughout the book and helps us to understand human identity and intelligence, health and illness, market behaviour and environmental protection, and people's reaction to risks and hazards.

A common assumption made by many people is that we (and for that matter all species) are in some way structured by our biology (our inner nature). We are born, we live and we die as a result of the genetic inheritance we have received from our parents and, more generally, from millions of years of evolution. Now, in some senses it would be facile to try to deny that each of us is equipped with different sets of possibilities, and we are undoubtedly, from time to time, constrained by our biological inheritance. It is certain that each of us will die. However, as Wendy Hollway suggested in Chapter 1, it would also be far too simplistic, and at the same time politically questionable, to suggest that we are biological machines living out a preprogrammed life over which we have little or no control. In suggesting this, we would be in danger of underestimating the role that our social and natural environments play in deciding whether or not and how a gene works. Furthermore, we would also neglect to say anything of the ways in which human beings (like all species) play a role in shaping those environments. As the biologist Steven Rose puts it, 'Organisms ... are far from passive – not just we humans, but all other living forms as well – are active players in their own futures' (1997, p.141). This sense of the active also gives us room to explore the *politics* of agency and structure. If structures do not wholly determine what we do and who we are, then we open up the possibility for changing things. This does not mean the human mind can escape its biological, cultural, material and social settings, but it does mean that those settings are not necessarily fixed and there will be possibilities for different forms of action. Bringing the social and natural together, then, helps us to unhinge both realms from the language of fixity whilst recognizing that neither offers us unending sources of possibility.

In the same way that our inner nature both constrains and enables human action (demonstrating that agency and structure are always dependent upon one another), so too do outer nature and society. We saw, for example, in Chapter 2, how our health was structured in complex ways by our biology interacting with social matters such as race, class, place, income, housing, and general well-being. Such structures are not fixed, so Brenda Smith and David Goldblatt explored some of the ways in which they offered political resources for dealing with health and ill-health. The interrelations between agency and structure were readily apparent in Chapter 3. As economic agents actively respond to price signals, so a market emerges which not only shapes future actions (it acts as a strongly influential structure) but also enables change and innovation (more agency). So the question is posed, can markets allow us to innovate in such a way as to build an environmentally less risky future? For Sue Himmelweit and Roberto Simonetti the jury has to be out, because markets both enable and constrain. Markets offer, through the price mechanism, some of the most promising means for dealing with environmental degradation. Adjusting the money values placed, or not placed, on the environment could help to shift priorities and remove the tendency to treat nature as an external aspect of economic affairs. But, at the same time, markets confine us to what seem to be some politically unassailable positions. The more we place monetary values on nature, the more the world (and more of the world) becomes subject to the dictates of economic rules and distributions. How environments will respond to being structured in this way is a matter for intense political debate. Finally, Chapter 4 warned against treating outer nature as an absolute structure that would allow us to ignore the role of human agency in the production of environmental disasters. If the social and natural are entangled, then human responsibility for vulnerability cannot be so easily ignored.

Uncertainty and diversity

In terms of our individual and species characteristics, of our health and welfare, of the outcomes of economic growth and expanding markets, and of the political effects of scientific knowledge, we live in a world that is so diverse that we may increasingly feel less than certain of our place in and understanding of that world. In the diverse and complex natural and social world that has been traced in the chapters in this book, we would expect a problem with any account of that world which gave the impression that the world behaved in straightforward ways.

So, to take an example from our understanding of human health, it is often unclear why some people develop particular diseases, such as cancers. As Chapter 1 showed, what is understood as human nature has changed significantly over time. Who do we blame when things go wrong like this? In the past we might have blamed a god or just fate. Now we look to employers, polluters, regulators, food manufacturers, the health service, or more broadly the general production system, capitalism and so on. Governments sometimes ask us to blame only ourselves (see Chapter 2).

What is apparent is that once we have mixed up the social and the natural, blame does not sit comfortably in inner nature, outer nature or in many of our social institutions. This is one reason for the protracted battles involving various experts who will try to convince you that 'their' department was not responsible or that we should be looking at so-and-so for an explanation. All of this buck-passing and finger-pointing is of course the stuff on which the media thrive, and so we are all increasingly drawn into a world where counter-claim succeeds claim, and precedes another claim. As we are drawn in, so we start to catch glimpses of what it might be like to live in a risk society (see Chapters 2 and 4).

As social scientists we can try to work with, rather than ignore, diversity and uncertainty. In Chapter 4, Steve Hinchliffe suggested through the BSE example that such diversity can make us suspicious of overly simplistic accounts of the social and natural world. We can be critical of those people who claim undue certainty. However, we can also use some powerful social science techniques to counter the claims of people who would use the idea of diversity and uncertainty to obscure their role in the making of events. Statistics, models and critical reading of texts and arguments are all part of the social scientists' toolkit. They allow us to build up complex accounts of society at the same time as affording a view of social and natural processes that allows us to be aware of the uneven distribution of power in society. As the authors of Chapter 3 demonstrated, it is sometimes useful to construct models of the world in order to understand some of the ways in which processes operate. Through their market model, Sue Himmelweit and Roberto Simonetti provide us with the tools to understand some of the important relationships that make a market work. In doing so, we start to understand some of the means by which markets affect distributions of costs and benefits. As the authors make clear, whilst we should never forget the limitations of the model, its understandings do help us to think in sophisticated ways about the necessary market or non-market policies for dealing with environmental degradation. It is important to emphasize the way their method works by first of all simplifying the world (the basis of the model) and then making the model progressively more complex. This can be contrasted with the ways in which politicians have used laboratory science, which were critiqued by Steve Hinchliffe in Chapter 4. In this case, the simplifications of the laboratory were treated too readily as the 'truth' and not enough care was taken when the model of disease and risk was to be used in a more complex natural and social world. In short, we constantly need to check that our models and the knowledge that we produce are relevant to the diverse and uncertain world in which we live.

Knowledge and knowing

Throughout the chapters in this book we have been sketching a world that is constituted from mixtures of social and natural matters. We have also tended to highlight the importance of *interrelationships* between nature and society as a way of explaining issues as diverse as human nature, health, risk and economies. So what constitutes human nature and health are matters of social and natural inheritance (genes and class, bodies and cultures). Economies work by setting up particular relationships between society (internal) and nature (largely external). If we accept this version of the world (and it should be noted that it is far from being uncontested), then this will have effects on the ways in which we need to engage with the world. In other words, if the natural and social worlds are no longer best seen as separate matters, then this poses some challenges to our ways of understanding the world, our theories and our methods.

The first challenge is that we need to be able develop ways of seeing the world that refuse to purify that world into social units. Thus, economists need to be wary of those economic models (like the dominant neo-classical model) that tend to ignore environmental degradation. As we saw in Chapter 3, as soon as we relax the assumptions of the model, markets become much more than relationships between producers and consumers. Therefore, other economists have attempted to build new models, a task that has led to the establishment of new sub-disciplines (including environmental and ecological economics). Psychologists too need to acknowledge the historical and spatial specificity of what we call human nature (Chapter 1).

The second challenge is that social scientists need to be ready to take on those who would have us believe that the world is reducible to natural units. Throughout this book, the authors have largely agreed that we cannot understand human behaviour, human nature, health, economy or risk by referring *solely* to the internal physical or chemical properties of a substance. We have already made this argument for genes and health in this Afterword, so I will finish by reiterating the point on risk that was presented in Chapter 4. To understand the hazard or danger of a substance it is important not only to understand something of its chemical, biological and physical attributes, it is also vital to understand its social life – where it gets used, what people do with it, what they want from it, if the users know the consequences of misuse, if the dangers are explained, how often it is used.

Without the two sides of the coin, the natural *and* the social, we will end up with inappropriate knowledge. To say that something is safe on the basis of chemical properties alone is to invite disaster (partly because a grossly simplified social world *is* being assumed for any such statement). As social scientists, we need to be mindful of how to build up evidence that will allow us to understand both the social and the natural. In order to do so, we will need to broaden our understanding of who is the expert and what counts as knowledge in our societies. This and other challenges are taken up by **Hughes and Fergusson (2004)**, who look in more detail at the ways in which social institutions shape and are being reshaped in contemporary society.

References

Hughes, G. and Fergusson, R. (eds) (2004) *Ordering Lives: Family, Work and Welfare* (2nd edn), London, Routledge/The Open University.

Latour, B. (1993) *We Have Never Been Modern*, London and New York, Harvester Wheatsheaf.

Rose, S. (1997) *Lifelines: Biology, Freedom, Determinism*, Harmondsworth, Penguin.

Acknowledgements

Grateful acknowledgement is made to the following sources for permission to reproduce material in this book.

Introduction

Figure 2: Ian Clifford Lott/Environmental Images.

Chapter 1

Figures

Figure 1.1: © The British Library; Figure 1.2: © The British Library; Figure 1.3: © Cambridge University Library; Figure 1.5: © Archaeological Service, Suffolk County Council; Figure 1.6: © State Museum Berlin/Bildarchive Preussischer Kulturbesitz.

Chapter 2

Figures

Figure 2.1: © Health Education Authority. Reproduced with permission; Figure 2.2: Hellier Mason/Still Pictures; Figure 2.3: Mary Evans Picture Library; Figure 2.4: Science Museum/Science and Society Picture Library; Figure 2.5: Cover from Hindley, J. and King, C. (1975) *How Your Body Works*, Usborne Publishing Ltd, London, reproduced with permission.

Table

Table 2.1: *Mortality Statistics, Perinatal and Infant: Social and Biological Factors, 1978–79 and 199,* (1995) Office for National Statistics. © Crown Copyright is reproduced with the permission of the Controller of Her Majesty's Stationery Office.

Chapter 3

Figures

Figure 3.1: adapted from MacGillivray, A. (1994) *Environmental Measures: Indicators for the UK Environment,* New Economics Foundation; Figure 3.3:

Mike Levers/Open University; Figure 3.4: A. Maslennikov/Still Pictures; Figure 3.5: Mark Edwards/Still Pictures.

Cartoons

p.99: © Dickinson/Punch; p.109: © Albert/Punch.

Chapter 4

Text

Elliott, L. (1998) 'A tale of two catastrophies', *The Guardian*, 7 November 1998, © Guardian Newspapers Ltd.

Figures

Figure 4.1: Stan Gamester/Environmental Images; Figure 4.2: Northampton Press Agency; Figure 4.3: Nick Cobbing/Still Pictures; Figure 4.4: Bell, S. (1988) *If. ... Breezes In*, Methuen, © Steve Bell 1987 & 1988; Figure 4.5 (left): Mitch Jacobson/Associated Press; Figure 4.5 (right): Oswaldo Rivas/ Popperfoto; Figure 4.6a (top): Jorgen Schytte/Still Pictures; Figures 4.6a (bottom), 4.6b and 4.8: Nigel Dickinson/Still Pictures; Figure 4.7: Bert Hardy/ Hulton Getty Picture Collection; Figure 4.9: Pete Addis/Environmental Images.

Cover

Image copyright © 1996 PhotoDisc, Inc.

Every effort has been made to trace all copyright owners, but if any has been inadvertently overlooked, the publishers will be pleased to make the necessary arrangements at the first opportunity.

Index